HOLLER AT YOUR DREAMS

for all of us.

Holler at Your Dreams™ Dangerously Inspiring Ideas for the Wildly Dope Soul™ Copyright © 2025 by Judi Holler
All rights reserved.

No part of this book may be reproduced, distributed, or transmitted in any form or by any means, including photocopying, recording, or other electronic or mechanical methods, without prior written permission from the publisher, except in the case of brief quotations embodied in critical reviews and certain other noncommercial uses permitted by copyright law.

ISBN: 978-1-7348250-8-4 (paperback)
ISBN: 978-1-7348250-9-1 (ebook)

Published by HOLLA! Worldwide
www.judiholler.com

Design and Creative Direction by Judi Holler
Illustrations and Cover Design by Ginger Hamilton
Cover image and select art photography by Jennifer Perkins
Back cover image by Claudia Johnstone

ATTENTION SCHOOLS AND BUSINESSES:
This book is available at quantity discounts with bulk purchase for educational, business, or sales promotional use. For information please email the HOLLA! Worldwide special sales department at hello@judiholler.com.

*this book was written by a human

STREET CRED

"This book is unapologetically Judi. And it had to be. You can't write a book that dares us to be our truest, boldest selves if we can't find your truth behind the words. No issue here. Judi doesn't just reveal her bruises—she turns each bash into a bash. Each scar into a celebration. Each bruise into a breakthrough. With every poem, lesson, and story, we're handed permission: to voice our own magenta, to live our neon, to laud the loudness of our truth. Her words don't just speak. They flow. They sing. They holler. And they ask us not just to receive them—but to embody them. To let her holler awaken our own, until our lives can't help but holler back."
—**Sekou Andrews, Grammy-Nominated Poet, Speaker & Thought Leader**

"Judi finds us standing in the doorway between the desire to be seen exactly as we are—and the fear of being seen like that. She pushes us through that door with a well-intentioned kick in the ass I'd call imaginaction: turning the version of yourself that only you've seen in your mind's eye into something the world can finally feel and respond to. She knows firsthand that the other side of thinking about it... is being about it."
—**Ken Black, Former VP of Design Future at Nike and Creative Director**

"Holler at Your Dreams isn't just a book—it's a soul-charged manifesto. It pulses with raw truth, luminous art, and language that dares you to remember who you are. From pain to paradigm shifts, this work cracks you wide open and gently guides you back home to yourself. As a fan and believer in all things Judi Holler, I'm beyond honored to witness its magic."
—**Naya Tapper, USA Olympian & Bronze Medalist**

"Holler at Your Dreams will help you punch through the doubt and discomfort that's been holding you back—so you can break out, break through, and break the mold. It's not just a book. It's a manifesto for doing the thing you've been dreaming about."
—**Alison Levine, NYT Bestselling Author of On the Edge, Team Captain, First American Women's Everest Expedition, Faculty, Thayer Leadership at West Point**

"This book is electric. It's not just a read, it's a reawakening. Every page is soaked in soul, truth, and that bold creative fire only YOU can bring. It lit me up!"
—**Vanessa Van Edwards, Harvard University Instructor, Bestselling Author, and Founder of ScienceofPeople.com**

STREET CRED

"This book isn't just a pep talk—it's a portal. Judi Holler cracked the code on turning pain into power and creativity into currency. Holler at Your Dreams will pull you out of your scroll hole and place the pen—and your power—back in your hand."
—**Jessica Zweig, National Bestselling Author, Serial Entrepreneur, and Host of The Spiritual Hustler Podcast**

"If you've ever felt like you're too much or not enough, this book will meet you right where you are—and wildly call you back to yourself. For anyone who's struggled with self-sabotage, following through, or a world that keeps asking you to tone it down, Judi's words are a guide back to your power, your voice, and your truth. This isn't about perfection or people-pleasing—it's about radical self-trust, creative courage, and honoring every version of who you've been while stepping fully into the light of who you are becoming."
— **Tanya Markul, Poet and author of "The She Book"**

"This book doesn't just whisper change, it dares you to burn what no longer fits, and honestly I wouldn't expect anything less from Judi! With soul and grit, it peels back the layers of false success, approval addiction, and old identities that no longer serve us. It's raw, real, and unapologetically honest - a mirror and a fire - calling you out and casting you forward. A spiritual reckoning for anyone brave enough to flip the f*ck it switch and step into who they're actually meant to be."
—**Maddison Ciccone, Master SoulCycle Instructor and Podcast Host**

"Sensational. Bold. Tender. Courageous. Judi Holler's explosively loving heart radiates off the page. She is a force of hope, a powerhouse of truth, an awakener of dreams. Her words are medicine for the soul. Her poetic lyricism, the warm embrace of her stories, and the radical truth of her wisdom ignite us—and can be felt in every single line she writes. The world needs Judi Holler."
—**Allison Massari, Hall of Fame Keynote Speaker, Celebrated Artist and Entrepreneur**

"Watching Judi bring this book to life has been nothing short of inspiring—and personal. Her words feel like a mirror, a megaphone, and a hug all at once. Holler at Your Dreams is more than a book—it's a permission slip to stop shrinking, own your magic, and go all in on the life you were meant to live."
—**Angie Smith, CEO, InVision**

STREET CRED

"This isn't just a book—it's an awakening. A bold, beautiful invitation to reconnect with the most creative, courageous parts of yourself. Judi Holler channels her genius with raw honesty, magnetic energy, and soul-stirring wisdom. This is your permission slip to remember who you really are. Buckle up, Queen. Your breakthrough starts now."
—Tali Kogan, Founder of MALKARI Jewelry and Transformational Stylist for Women

"This one's staying on my nightstand forever. Judi delivers a heart-to-heart with the bravest version of yourself—honest, unfiltered, and exactly what you need when you're done chasing gold stars and outside approval. She guides us through the fear and resistance that keep us small, and reminds us what it means to fully express who we are."
—Carrie Campbell, SVP, Boston Red Sox

"Judi has always been a source of inspiration—but this book is something more. Holler at Your Dreams is a powerful tool for transformation. You can feel her heart on every page as she shares the power of owning your truth, claiming your peace, standing in your power, and moving forward with bold purpose. Bravo, my girl!"
—Kirsten Ferguson, Peloton Instructor, Motivational Speaker & Professional Mood Booster

HOLLER AT YOUR DREAMS
Dangerously Inspiring Ideas for the Wildly Dope Soul

JUDI HOLLER

Nothing in this book is fact—
only what I've learned to be true.

This book is a collection, a manifesto, a map.

A mixtape of thoughts, ideas, downloads, prayers, poems,
serendipity, mojo, miracles, and reflections
that have helped me move through debilitating anxiety, fear,
jealousy, insecurity, anger, uncertainty, reinvention, and change.

Some of these ideas may hit home.
Others may not.
Take what serves you—leave the rest.

Think of each idea as an invitation.
To stop playing small.
To stop fearing change.
To keep your power.
To trust yourself.
To be yourself.
To free yourself.
To express yourself.

And most importantly—
to come back home to yourself.

Also by Judi Holler:

Fear is My Homeboy
The #FearBoss Project

For all my angels, on earth and beyond.

For Scott, who always brings me back home, to myself, with these three words:
Just Be You.

To endings that shape us,
To beginnings that call,
To the divine design of time—guiding us through it all.

THE PLAYLIST

21   **FOREWORD**
by Jade Simmons

23   **INTRODUCTION**
Author's Note and How to Use This Book

26   **THE PAIN**
Feel it

120   **THE PEACE**
Accept it

212   **THE PRESENCE**
Be it

309   **THE PARADIGM**
Transcend it

405   **SNAPS**
Acknowledgements and Gratitude

PASS THE MIC

foreword by Jade Simmons

Trust and believe—if you're reading this right now, it means you're on the verge. You are on the brink of a new era that has your name written all over it. Future You has been celebrating this day for a while now. She never doubted it would come—the day the biggest, boldest version of yourself would show up armed, empowered, and equipped to take the most consequential leap of your life.

And truthfully? It's much bigger than a leap. You've taken leaps before. You've survived.

This? This is a freefall in faith—the kind that only comes after years of trying, doing, failing, succeeding, and tracking your own growth. You've more than made the grade, a thousand times over. This era is about building belief in the power of simply being. And there's no better guide than the brave, shape-shifting queen herself—Judi Holler.

Here's the thing: Judi arrives in the most pristine packaging—everything she touches is gorgeous, bold, and as cool as it gets. She and her team? They never miss. And then, just when you think she's unreachable, she does the wildest thing: she lays out exactly what she's gotten wrong. She intentionally shatters the illusion of perfection so you won't get tripped up by it. That's the kind of leader you want guiding you through reinvention—someone who's always in the middle of it. Unapologetic is the address you want to get to—and Judi? She already lives there.

She and I both know from experience: the world will try to convince you to do more. But purpose isn't about doing—though yes, incredible things happen when you do what you do. Purpose is freed when you are being all of yourself, all of the time—fully aware of the impact you've always had. If you're living powerfully, life will constantly call you to shed the skin of the last season. Don't fear letting go of the scaly stuff—because underneath is an irreplicable new design. You'll still be you—but it will be the version uniquely called to make waves in this new era. Transformation is about to become your new middle name. Wear it proudly.

Make no excuses for your metamorphosis.
You do not owe anyone your sameness.

Keep your ears tuned to the next—because the now only lasts as long as it needs. And even with all the change you're about to embrace, believe me when I say: There is a new space ahead where you get to wake up and simply exist.

Not only will you awaken to a sense of peace and the deep knowing that God created you for such a time as this, but you will find that suddenly you have become profoundly necessary

Before now, you may have felt like a luxury. An ornament. A prospect. Someone's maybe. Someone's quota. Someone's second choice. An industry's momentary sweetheart. An oddity one could take or leave. But not in this new era. Here, you are an absolute. Freefall into the truth that in this season, you are a person of sheer consequence—an essential presence in the world around you.

You do not wait to be discovered. You discover yourself.
You do not wait to be chosen. You were born chosen.
You do not beg for a thing. You declare a thing—and if it's in alignment with who you were created to be, then baby, it's already done.

So go. Freefall into all of the above.

Breathe.
Believe.
Buckle up.

INTRODUCTION

Friends,

If we haven't met, allow me to introduce myself. My name is Judi Holler, and the ideas in this book? They brought me back home—to myself.

I got to a place where I was lost, angry, anxious, afraid—and carrying a major chip on my shoulder. It was a me-against-the-world vibe, sending dangerous signals to the universe that I wasn't worthy of the greatness I craved. Drowning in doubt, I started writing checks to buy my way back. And while others were cashing in on my insecurities, I was going soul bankrupt.

Then one Sunday, right in the middle of my madness, I drove to Barnes & Noble. I bought a stack of blank notebooks, a few poetry books, children's books in verse, and a fresh set of pens. That afternoon, I started writing again. My aim was to check myself, hype myself, remind myself—find myself. But before I knew it, the words became something more. I was creating my way out of the darkness. And as my word count soared, so did my self-esteem.

I began working on myself, with myself, through myself. Yes, I met incredible healers and earth angels along the way—but no coach, course, or shaman saved me. My self-expression did. Writing, poetry, art, music, movement and creativity became my way back home. And in that process, I realized the truth:

Expressionism isn't exclusive to art—we are the art.

So, spirit moved me to create a new form of art called Self-Expressionism™—a bold, soul-driven self-leadership philosophy built for the future of work, and life: unlocking creativity, originality, and initiative from the inside out.

We are living inside a creative revolution—one that will be bigger than the industrial revolution.

But we're also facing a creative crisis—where fear, comparison, and the algorithm have gotten louder than our own rhythm.

We're so stuck in the scroll, we can't hear our soul.

And what feels cringe?
Is usually just unexpressed self-envy.

People don't hate that you're expressive.
They hate that they've silenced themselves.

This book is a personal collection of everything I created to unsilence myself—to climb out of doubt, comparison, anxiety, and the fear of my own voice. Consider it your roadmap home—a guide to unlocking your potential, trusting your rhythm, and becoming your own greatest creation.

One thing I know for sure is this: The greatest masterpiece of all time is the canvas of your life. Now it's time to pick up the brush and start painting. So grab my hand and let me lead the way— we've been waiting for you.

You know what time it is—time to holler at your one, dope, wildly precious soul.

Made with Love.

xx

HOW TO USE THIS BOOK

This book isn't just a book—it's a creative companion, a vibe check, and an oracle all in one. Inside, you'll find 365 original ideas—poetry, prose, verse, downloads, stories, ideas, and quotes—to keep you inspired every step of the way. Think of it as 365 days and ways to holler at your dreams.

READ IT FRONT TO BACK.
If you want the full experience, read it straight through. This book is a journey back home to yourself—starting with feeling the pain, accepting what is, stepping into who you were born to be, and then taking it all to the next level with your newfound alignment.

LET THE PAGE BE A PORTAL.
One of my all-time favorite things to do is pull a book off my shelf, close my eyes, and flip through the pages until I feel the right moment to stop. When I open my eyes, I trust that whatever words I land on are exactly what I need to hear. I dare you to use this book the same way. Got a question? Feeling stuck? Need a sign from the universe? Ask. Flip. Stop. Read. Trust.

THIS AIN'T YA AVERAGE BOOKSTORE FIND.
Some of the best books I've ever found were discovered in chic little independent shops —the kind of books you stumble upon while traveling, sipping a latte, or digging through treasures with your bestie. That's the energy of this book. Boutique, not basic.

EVEN WHEN IT'S JUST SITTING THERE...
The spine was designed to be a visual battle cry—a neon sign for your soul. Even if you let it collect dust, just seeing the spine of this book sitting on your shelf will remind you to keeping hollering at your dreams.

THE GIFT THAT KEEPS HOLLERING!
Gift giving is my love language and I'm always looking for the perfect gift so I wanted to make it. This book was designed to be your new favorite gift to give. So grab a stack, wrap 'em up, and make it rain like it's Oprah's Favorite Things. "YOU GET A BOOK! YOU GET A BOOK! EVERYBODY GETS A BOOK!"

There's no wrong way to use this book. Well, actually, I guess there's only one. Not using it at all.

Let's dive in.
Your soul is waiting.

THE PAIN

"THERE IS GOING TO BE TURBULENCE AS YOU SHIFT FROM ONE UNIVERSE TO ANOTHER."
LALAH DELIA

(FEEL IT)

Pain is the threshold between what was and what could be. It is the turbulence that shakes us loose from old ways of thinking, being, and believing. And yet, we often resist it, treating discomfort like a stop sign instead of a portal.

But pain is intelligence. It carries messages, directions, breakthroughs. It does not come to break you; it comes to wake you.

In this section, we meet pain head-on—not as an enemy, but as an invitation. We learn to decode its wisdom, honor its lessons, and move through it with faith instead of fear. We stop outsourcing our power to what the world expects and start trusting our own map.

This is where the shift begins.

PAIN IS THE BEGINNING
OF YOUR BECOMING.

THE SWEET SURRENDER
OF NO LONGER RUNNING.

LET THE PAIN PAINT

Pain doesn't just break us—it builds us. But only if we let it move. One of the most powerful things you can do with your pain is make something out of it. It's Self-Expressionism in action. Because around here? We don't hustle and stress.

We hustle and flow.

While I've been writing the book you're reading my whole life—nearly five decades of wisdom and wake-up calls—it all truly began with a trip to Barnes & Noble. I wandered through the poetry section, filling my basket with books, notebooks, colored pencils, and pens. I didn't have a plan, but I had a gut feeling I needed to start writing again. I was untethered. Unsure how to put words to what I was feeling—this inner knowing I was becoming—and without anyone's permission, I anointed myself a poet. Woke up that beast. That inner rhythmic raptress who had been lying dormant.

So I wrote. And wrote. And wrote. And wrote.

Sometimes I'd pull over on the side of the road, scribbling lyrics and bars on Starbucks egg white wrappers so I wouldn't lose the download coming through. I sketched. I rapped. I rhymed. I let my pain paint something. And little by little, it set me free. I created my way out of the chaos—and into my next evolution.

Art can do that. Creation gives chaos a container.

Whether it's listening to music or making a playlist, writing poetry or recording intuitive voice memos (I wrote a lot of this book that way—dope downloads would hit while driving), throwing paint on a canvas or scribbling in a journal—when you make something from your ache, you move it from inside of you to outside of you.

You give it shape. You give it meaning. And eventually, you give it closure.

This isn't about being good at art. It's about letting your pain have a voice—so you don't become a victim to it.

DARKNESS ONLY BECOMES LIGHT,

WHEN YOU FLIP ON THE SWITCH.

Sometimes I have bad dreams about freezing—
publicly seizing.
Not physically,
but mentally.
It's like I have the words,
but they just won't come out—
a verbal drought.
A cracked-earth silence,
heat-waved in doubt.
Usually, I'm about to take a stage—
a big fancy one,
like the Oscars or the Grammys.
Red carpets galore,
and I'm scheduled to perform
original words I had written.
I should be smitten,
but instead I'm panic-stricken,
because what began as a masterpiece
makes me want to run for the streets.
As I completely blank out,
unable to find my voice,
confidence destroyed—
the stage now quicksand,
shame showing its hand.
My heart racing,
people backstage pacing,
disappointment quickly blazing
as I question this craving
I have for behaving
like I deserve to be amazing.
I'm quickly fading
as I shake awake
with the daylight saving—
<me>
from having to see
what I couldn't be.
As I pour a coffee
and thank God
it was only just a dream.

ARE YOU ASLEEP?

Staying asleep isn't just about physical rest—it's about spiritual, mental, and emotional stagnation. It's living passively, moving through life on autopilot, waiting for someone else to tell you who you are, what you're worth, and what's possible for you. It's pressing snooze on your potential, your joy, your dreams.

Being asleep means avoiding responsibility—blaming others, the economy, your past, or your circumstances instead of owning your choices. It means fearing change—choosing comfort over courage, even when your comfort zone is suffocating you. It's the victim mindset—seeing yourself as powerless instead of stepping up as the creator of your life. It's excusing inaction—complaining, procrastinating, or waiting for the "right time" instead of showing up and doing the work. It's a lack of curiosity—refusing to ask questions, learn, or challenge outdated ways of thinking. It's conforming—following the crowd, doing what's expected, ignoring the pull toward something greater.

I know this because I've been asleep, too.

For years, I was sleeping on my poetry—on my ability to write in verse, to create rhythm with words, to express what I couldn't say out loud. My pen has power, but that doesn't mean it's pain-free. I write to set myself free. I write to feel it all. I write to release it all. Writing—whether in rhyme or freestyle—is my way of staying awake to myself. I have stacks on stacks of notebooks, each a journey back home to me. And that's the whole point of this creative process: to make sure I don't sleep on myself.

Most people don't even realize they're asleep. But if we want to wake up, we first have to understand what it means to be asleep—so we can do the inverse. So, how do you wake up? The answer? You have to be with yourself. No distractions. No noise. Just you.

It might not be poetry for you, but that doesn't mean you can't find your own way back home. Try journaling—no structure, no rules, just a stream of thoughts on the page. Ground yourself in nature. Take off your shoes, stand in the grass, and breathe. Take a break from social media. Step away for a day, a weekend, or longer. Go on a solo vacation or a day trip. Be your own best company. Take yourself on a creativity date—visit a museum, make art, explore something new. Drive in silence. No music. No podcasts. Just you and your thoughts. Sit in stillness. Meditate. Breathe. Listen.

Because here's the thing: you will never hear the voice of your soul if you don't turn down the noise.

There's this thing I do
after anything social
or new—
where I try to act fly,
cool as a blue sky.
But truthfully?
I'm spiraling inside.
Wondering—
Was I OK?
Was that OK?
Did I talk too much?
Did I listen enough?
Should I have been more chill?
Did I take up too much space?
Did I shine too bright?
I know—
these are just childhood echos.
Unhealed things.
Lessons I never asked for.
Conditioned to apologize for my presence.
To take the spotlight
and toss it in another direction
before it burned with rejection.
But now I know—
those are lies,
wrapped in the skin
of a ghost named perfection.
Because why should I have to dim my light
just to keep the peace
in rooms I was born to electrify?

YOU'LL NEVER GET IN THIS LIFE WHAT YOU AREN'T BRAVE ENOUGH TO *HOLLER* AT.

YUMA

Lately, I've been listening to a lot of Abraham Hicks—a collection of spiritual teachings channeled by Esther Hicks, focused on the law of attraction, mindset, and personal alignment. One story they tell often is about driving from San Diego to Phoenix, a route they take frequently for live events.

When they leave California, they plug Phoenix into their GPS. The system guides them exactly where to go. Along the way, they pass through Yuma, Arizona—about halfway between the two cities.

The lesson? Life works the same way.

If you're headed toward a destination—whether it's a goal, a dream, or the next version of yourself—it's going to take time. You'll see things along the way. You may need to stop for gas, grab food, or deal with an unexpected flat tire. There will be detours, good and bad, but you are on your way.

The problem? Most of us get stuck in Yuma.

We get impatient. We think it's taking too long. We compare our journey to someone else's and wonder why they seem to be arriving faster. We overthink, self-sabotage, and convince ourselves to turn around—when, in reality, if we had just pushed past Yuma, we would have made it.

I've done this more times than I can count.

Instead of trusting the process, I've gotten lost in the messy middle. I've doubted myself, questioned everything, and sent myself back to the starting line when I was probably inches from the breakthrough I was chasing.

It became a vicious cycle—reworking, overthinking, restarting—when all I needed to do was just keep going.

So, the moral of the story?

You're en route to your destination. There will be bumps. You'll have to stop and stretch. But whatever you do—don't get stuck in Yuma. Keep driving.

Bitterness
She wears me like a dress—
a result of stress,
and how I second-guess
each and every step,
spinning me up
in her delicate web.
Bitterness
The monster under my bed,
slowly crawling through my head,
watering seeds of resentment,
hoping they'll grow tall enough
to shield me from all this regret.
Bitterness
A graveyard of grudges,
a poison that paralyzes,
a jail of judgment,
a venomous asylum—
where dreams go to die.
Bitterness
I refuse to let her win.
As I climb over the walls she's built,
burying the grudges,
uprooting the weeds,
planting new seeds—
and I take back my peace.

NOT EVERY YEAR IS THE YEAR

Some years are meant for winning. Others are meant for wisdom.

2024 brought me to my knees. And while it won't go down as my favorite calendar year, it will go down as one of the most important—because it forced me to face things I might've kept outrunning. Slower seasons do that. They strip away the noise. They reveal what you've been avoiding. They show you what needs your attention.

So if you're walking through a year that feels more like a breakdown than a breakthrough, please know this: not every year is the year. And that doesn't mean you're off track.

Sometimes, it's the storm that reveals what needs to go.
Sometimes, it's the stillness that reminds you what really matters.
Sometimes, it's the pain that sharpens the purpose.

The culture will tell you to bounce back. To pivot. To stay positive. But what if you just felt it? What if you made space to grieve the version of life you thought you'd be living right now? What if you stopped judging your slow season and started seeing it as sacred?

Not every year is the year to bloom. But every year plants something.

Let this one grow you.

FED UP

I realized I've spent too much time over the years letting people who aren't me tell me how to be me. And that? That's what it looks like to give away your power. So, let's talk about the rules. The systems. The structure. The silent code that says:

"This is how it's done."
"You can't do that."
"That's too much."
"Be more like this."
"Tone it down."
"Play it safe."

Sound familiar?

There's this invisible pressure—especially in the keynote speaking world—to be palatable. To be "safe enough" for the homepage. To sound like everyone else so you can be trusted by boardrooms full of people you may never meet. But here's the problem: the whole reason I got into this game was because I didn't know better. Because I was bold. Audacious. A little delulu. Because I had something to say—and I said it. And now, here I am, diluting my edge just to be "bookable"? Nah.

So I made a decision: I'm done shrinking.

I recently gave my brand a lil' remix. Not just a polish—a truth-telling upgrade. I decided to tell the real story of who I am, what I do, who I serve, and who I'm not for. Yes, I still have the timeless speaker assets—great video, strong stage presence, clear takeaways, client logos, and keynote content that solves real problems. But I also let the real me show up. Because what's the point of having a "safe" website if people book you for someone you're not?

Wouldn't you rather walk into a room already being loved for who you are than trying to fit into who they hoped you'd be?

I'm done selling myself to people who aren't buying anyway. So I might as well be myself.

Whether you're a speaker, a CEO, an artist, a parent, or a project manager... this applies. You are not your job title. You are not just what you do. You are the originality inside of it. And if we're entering a world where AI can mimic tone, write code, and replicate voices... then the only thing that will ever be original is the soul that only you carry because it's the one thing AI will never have, a soul.

So they may try to clip your wings. Call you "too much." Dismiss you. Dull you. But here's the white hot truth: The "cringe" others feel is often just unexpressed self-envy.

People don't hate that you're expressive.
They hate that they've silenced themselves.

For so long,
I thought something was wrong—
with me,
with who I came to be,
with how I see,
myself,
the future,
and everything else.
Because I'd go out into the world,
light it on fire,
then come home
and feel so alone.
Yes, it's my family—
so why do they feel like strangers?
At times, I feel so much anger.
But mostly,
I need to crawl out of this container.
I can't breathe in here.
I can't be in here.
I can't see in here.
But thank Goddess, I can see out there.
Because I see joy.
I see love.
I see abundance.
I see mothers—
mothers who actually mother,
reminding me there's another way
of being.
of seeing.
of doing.
So I surrender to the tidal
W A V E
of feeling tribal—
of becoming my own bible,
devoted to being a disciple
of
breaking the cycle.

OPPOSITE OF HER

What if your pain is where your originality lives? What if the thing you've been trying to hide, fix, or outrun is actually the key to your voice, your truth, your power?

I've learned this firsthand. My relationship with my mother has been a wound, a mirror, and—more than anything—a muse. Paradoxically, there hasn't been much of a relationship at all. And for a long time, that hurt. Deeply. But now, as I approach 50, I've moved from anger into something more freeing: gratitude. Because if I'd had a squeaky-clean, picture-perfect relationship with my mom, I wouldn't be the woman I am today.

I live the way I do—bold, awake, creative, self-expressed—because I chose to break the cycle. And yes, I've got grace for her generation. They didn't have the tools we have now. But I also know my mom had a really hard life. And while I'm sorry for that—truly—I also believe this: we still have a responsibility to clean up our mess. If we don't, we pass it down. Especially if we choose to have kids.

It doesn't mean we have to be perfect. But when we ignore our trauma, our childhood wounds, or our pain, we don't eliminate it—we just manifest it somewhere else. And let me tell you, unprocessed trauma doesn't vanish. It leaks out. In anxiety. In rage. In addiction. In projection. In how we love and how we fight.

In my house growing up, conflict resolution didn't exist. Calm wasn't a thing. Most arguments ended with a lamp shattered or a fist through the drywall. It was scary. And the worst part? That became normal. That was the standard.

I knew I wanted something different. And I've been shaping that reality on purpose, piece by piece, day by day.

My mother isn't a role model. She's a reflection. A warning. A reminder of what happens when we don't deal with our pain. And because of that, she's also become one of my greatest muses. The fuel for my fire. The mirror that keeps me awake. The reason I fight for peace, creativity, expression, and freedom—not just for myself, but for every person I speak to and stand beside.

You don't have to glamorize your suffering to learn from it. But if you're willing to look it in the eye—to really get honest—you might see that the thing you thought disqualified you is actually the exact thing that made you different. The crack is where the originality lives. The pain becomes the path.

Let it.

I no longer let
the disease to please
bring me to my knees.
Instead, I climb to the top of the trees
so I can feel the breeze—
and really see
what I couldn't at the bottom,
through the leaves:
An infinity
of possibility,
daring me,
asking me,
telling me—
to put down the weight of what isn't mine.
Because someone else's dark night
doesn't have to be my life.
So I close my eyes
at the top of this tree,
allowing the breeze to help me see
what I couldn't at the bottom,
through the leaves—
that my one wild, precious life
is always up to me.

ON PEOPLE PLEASING

You can't trick people into liking you. And not everybody is going to. Honestly? If everybody likes you, it's a pretty good indicator that you're playing it way too safe. Because if you're for everyone, you're for no one.

The problem is, we spend so much time worrying about being disliked, made fun of, or judged. But here's the cold, hard truth: people already don't like you. They're already judging you. They're already talking about you behind your back.

So the real question is: who are you living for? You—or everyone else? You—or strangers on the internet you'll never even meet?

Let's flip the script, shall we? Because if people are already talking...
Let's go give 'em something to talk about.

Can I get a HOLLA for that one?

If you feel like you're constantly selling yourself, maybe it's time to stop selling—and start being yourself. Because nobody really cares about your pitch deck, your bullet points, or your fancy website. And we can all tell the difference between something memorized and something meant.

It's not about persuasion. It's about soul. And people feel your essence. If it's good—if it's true—that's what draws them in. It's your vibe. Your enthusiasm. Your presence. All of that gets translated into the things you make.

When people buy something, it's because it speaks to them. So—speak to us. What's your perspective? What have you lived through? What's your story? What wisdom have you earned? What's your take?

It's like the wave at a baseball game—the old-school kind that starts in one section, builds momentum, and then ripples through the whole stadium. That's what your enthusiasm does. That's what being you does. It creates a wave of magic that not only inspires others to do the same—but helps you find your people faster.

So stop worrying about being liked.
Be the wave.

FEAR FEAR LESS

Let me be real with you: I hate the word fearless.

I know the intent behind it is good—we're trying to talk about courage and strength. But fearless sends the wrong message. It whispers that if you feel fear, something's wrong with you. That maybe you're not brave enough. Not strong enough. Not ready enough.

And that is a lie.

Here's what I've come to know—if you're feeling fear, it probably means you're on the right track. It means you're standing at the edge of growth. It means you're about to do something new. Become someone new. Expand into a version of yourself you haven't met yet.

Of course it's going to feel uncomfortable. Of course it's going to feel scary. That doesn't make you weak. That makes you human.

Bravery isn't the absence of fear. It's the movement in spite of it. It's going scared. Shaking —and showing up anyway. Stepping forward without knowing what's next.

I once heard someone say that fearless is a poison pretending to be a vitamin. I don't know who originally said it—but shout out to you, whoever you are. Because I never forgot it. And it's true: fear loves to show up in fancy disguises. It wraps itself in ambition or selflessness or "being realistic." But what looks good on the surface is often what's holding us back underneath.

Fearless.
Perfectionism.
Procrastination.
People-pleasing.
Overworking.
Excuse-making.
Martyrdom.

All of them? Poisons pretending to be vitamins.

So let's stop chasing fearless. Let's stop pretending we're not afraid.

Instead, let's focus on fearing our fear itself... less.
That's what makes you brave.

I'm really good at borrowing trouble, dress-rehearsing tragedy, busting my own proverbial bubble. Maybe it's entrepreneurship— the ups and downs, the ebbs and flows, the that's just the way it goes mindset, that has become the combined net of having a defined set of fears.

Perfectionism. Procrastination. Self-sabotage. Self-doubt. All fear's shadows, lurking near. But before it's too late, courage softly whispers in my ear— Psst. I know you're scared, that's quite clear. But don't you worry, the path is near, because all this fear is actually a mirror.

See, I finally figured out—fearless is a lie. Because if you're afraid, you're doing it right. Fear is my constant companion, my ride or die. It keeps me safe, sharp, alive, so I don't just survive— I thrive. And I don't know about you, but the only fearless people I know are sociopaths and five-year-olds.

No one gets out of life pain-free— Death and taxes, taking chances, making advances, dodging cancers. Around every corner, we need new armor, for battles we fight— inside, outside, bobbing, weaving, trying not to sink like a submarine or mask ourselves like it's Hollaween.

Costumes aside, I take pride in the fact that I have tried. Brave things. Big things. Bold things. Bad things. Scary things. Old things. New things. Dope things. Because is there anything scarier than missing your chance, or letting fear have the last dance?

So, personally, I'd rather keep my fear near— to remind me I'm here. Another day. Another chance.

It's guts over fear.

STAY READY

I want to save you some pain. Specifically, the pain of not knowing how to clearly communicate your value. Because if you can't pitch yourself—if you can't articulate who you are and what you do with clarity and confidence—you will miss opportunities. Period.

I learned this the hard way.

I was on a flight to the Bahamas for a speaking event, and this woman a few rows up leans over her seat, taps me on the knee, and says, "Hey—I overheard you say you're a keynote speaker. I'm Diana, SVP at [insert big company]. I actually need a speaker in two months—tell me what you speak about again?"

And y'all... I bombed.

I had been speaking professionally for years. But at the time, I was scattered. I wasn't trusting myself. I had lost my focus. And in that moment—right in front of a decision-maker—I could barely pitch what I did. I stumbled through it, totally disconnected. When the plane landed, I gathered my things. And there it was: the business card I had handed her—left on the seat, tossed out with her trash.

Ouch. But also... HOLLAlujah.

Because that moment woke me up. I got my $hit together. I remembered who I was. A boss. A talent. A pro. And I made a promise to never, ever let a moment like that pass me by again.

If you've ever been in that moment—or fear being in it—here's a fix to help you land the plane (pun intended):

The Swag Statement Framework:
I am a ────────────────────── (what you do)
Who helps ──────────────────── (target audience)
Understand or do ──────────────── (your expertise)
So they can ────────────────── (transformation you create)

Say it. Own it. Practice it. Because you will be asked. And when you are, you better be ready to answer like the boss you are.

Stay ready.

IN HERE.
It's so loud in here.
I can't hear in here.
I can't breathe in here.
I can't see in here.
I don't feel like me in here.
My thoughts don't believe in me in here.
How did I get in here?
Why can't I leave in here?
The walls are closing in in here.
My past still lives in here.
I'm carrying too much in here.
I'm tired of hiding in here.
I need to get out of here.
I want to scream in here.
I keep drowning in here.
But I need to dream in here.
So I whisper to God—can you meet me in here?

ON QUITTING

Most people don't quit because they can't handle the work—they quit because they mistake pressure for punishment. They think resistance means stop. But the truth is, pressure is often the final test before the transformation. Just ask any diamond. What makes it shine? Insane pressure. Without it, it's just a lump of carbon. Same goes for us.

Breakthroughs don't show up with warning signs or confetti. They usually look like fear. Like friction. Like failure. But here's the truth: there is no finish line. There's only the next level. The next layer. The next leap. The process is the whole freaking point.

I almost missed one of the biggest breakthroughs of my life because of that lie. When I first signed up for improv classes at Second City in Chicago, it was meant to be fun. A way to meet people. Something just for me. A dream I'd always wanted to manifest. But the pressure hit me hard.

It was Second City—iconic—so I told myself I had to be funny, smart, and really freaking good. But what if I wasn't? My entire walk from my apartment in Lincoln Park to that classroom in Old Town was a spiral of panic. I psyched myself out. I stood outside the door—and never walked in. I quit before the class even started. I didn't feel good enough. Didn't feel funny enough. Didn't feel young enough. I was 30 years old and convinced I was already too late. So I ran home, tail tucked, sure I'd missed my shot.

But something in me knew.

Two years later—after a lot of personal development and some loud, loving friends—I went back. And thank God I did. That one decision changed everything. It led to the stage. To my voice. To my work. To this.

So if you're standing in the hallway of "I can't do this," pause.

That pressure you're feeling?
It's not punishment. It's preparation.
Hold on. You're closer than you think.

As I write these words,
tears fill my eyes—
because I don't know who to trust.
Sometimes, it all feels like a lie.
When I can't pick up the phone
and call someone who truly knows—
how I feel,
what to say,
how to guide me through the gray—
it makes me feel so alone.
And I start to question—
this road I'm on,
this business I'm in,
this mission I have,
this vision I've mapped.
I know God has a plan,
but right now, I don't think I can
go any further
without a lifeline.
A rope.
Hope.
Because everything feels
so faux.
So I close my eyes,
take a deep breath,
and trust the divine whispers
that haven't failed me yet.
Because even in this moment of doubt,
I know—
the light will always find its way out.

NO LONGER GOOD

Have you ever looked around your life and thought, "Why does everything that used to feel good... not feel good anymore?" The conversations that once energized you now feel like a drain. The places you used to love? Meh. The people who used to get you? Now they don't even see you. The doors that used to fly open? Now they're creaking.

You're not crazy. You're leveling up. And as someone who is writing this book smack dab in the middle of a major personal shift, I want to speak directly to the discomfort—because here's what I've learned loud and clear: if you are not made uncomfortable, you will not move.

We are shaken so we wake up. We are poked so we pivot. We are pressed so we transform. It's like getting into your car in the middle of an Arizona summer, and your seat is so hot it literally burns your ass. You jump up. You move. You don't sit there and marinate—you react. Instantly. That's what transformation feels like. That's what this season feels like.

Here are seven things that happen when you're on the edge of your next level—straight from my own experience right now:

1. Friendships that used to feel like home no longer do. You love them, but the energy just isn't aligned.
2. Doors that used to fly open suddenly won't budge. What worked before doesn't work now.
3. Clients, projects, and people who once felt right feel... off. You can't explain it, but the vibe is off and the soul is saying "nope."
4. Environments that used to excite you feel flat. The party, the city, the job, the circle—it's just not it anymore.
5. Conversations you used to love now bore or irritate you. Surface talk won't cut it when you're deepening your own truth.
6. You feel internal turbulence you can't explain. Anxiety, exhaustion, bursts of clarity followed by fog. You're not broken—you're breaking through.
7. Your intuition is on fire. You see through fake energy, disingenuous offers, and performative behavior like never before—and you either feel instantly drawn in or immediately repelled.

This isn't burnout. It's becoming.
It's not the end. It's the edge.

And yes—some people will fall away. Not because you're wrong, but because you're becoming someone they no longer recognize—or worse, someone they're afraid to become. Your growth is a mirror. And not everyone is ready to look. This is where courage lives. This is the "hot seat in the car" moment of your life. And you've got two choices: Wait for it to cool off (and stay the same). Or jump out, move different, and trust what's next.

Because this isn't about applause. It's about alignment. So let this be a reminder that nothing is wrong with you. You're just leveling up. You're leaving old systems, small rooms, shallow conversations, and safe energy behind.

You're becoming.

She'll take courage on the rocks,
 with a dash of hard knocks—
    cause that's what unlocks
       all those chains on her box.

AM I DOING THIS RIGHT?

That's the question under almost every bold move we make. Am I doing it right? It's the whisper that haunts every pivot, every risk, every next-level leap. Because it's not the hustle or the grind that gets us—it's the uncertainty. It's the not knowing.

Most of us already understand that growth requires discomfort. We know we'll have to take ownership, face fear, make the leap—because no one's coming to save us. We get that. What we're really scared of is getting it wrong. Choosing the wrong path. Looking stupid. Wasting time. Losing something or someone. Feeling lost. Failing publicly.

But when that fear hits, I want you to remember this: you may not be 100% certain about the path, but you can be 100% certain about yourself. That's the shift. That's the vibe. And if you don't feel that self-certainty yet—here's how to get it.

Ask yourself:

What am I great at?
What am I not great at?
What do I value?
What do I not value?
What do I believe in?
What do I not believe in?
Who am I for?
Who am I not for?

This is how you get anchored. Because the goal isn't to eliminate uncertainty—it's to learn how to move through it with more confidence.

You may not know if you made the right choice, but you know who you are. You know what you believe. What you value. What lights you up. What you're not willing to compromise.

You may not be sure about the solution—but you can always trust the solver.

If you didn't have your $hit,
would you still be
THA $HIT?
If you didn't have your pain,
would your gains still feel like gains?
You shouldn't have to explain
why you choose to maintain
a level of pain
so you don't remain
in the same place you were last year.
And isn't that what we should all really F E A R?
Staying the same.
Instead of making it rain,
dropping into new domains,
going against the grain,
popping bottles like champagne,
trekking new terrain,
feeling no restrain.
For the breakthroughs that require breaking.
For the pain that makes us pay attention
For the $hit that makes us THA $HIT.
We don't complain—
we commit.
Legit.
    Too legit
        To ever quit.

CEASE & DESIST

Let me tell you a story I've never shared before. It's equal parts humiliating, infuriating, and transformational. It taught me one of the biggest lessons of my life: life is always happening for you, even when it feels like it's trying to destroy you.

So here's the tea. Before I became the Fear Is My Homeboy girl—before I built a keynote speaking business teaching people how to reframe fear—I was giving talks on personal branding.

Picture me in 2008, running around Chicago with a FlipCam, filming content to create FOMO and grow membership in my industry association. I'd race home, upload the footage to Facebook (OG Instagram Stories, people!), and hustle my way into becoming the personal branding "it girl." Eventually, I created a talk called Personal Branding, Improvised. I slapped a catchy hashtag on it, built a little following, and thought I was the moment.

Judi Booty was vibing.

Then one summer day in 2014, I opened my mailbox to find a letter that changed everything: a cease-and-desist. I froze. My heart raced. My palms went full-on sprinkler mode. My first thought? Welp, this is it. I'm a fraud, a criminal, and my next keynote will be from county jail.

A stranger in California had allegedly trademarked the hashtag I was using and wanted me to back off. She had lawyers. Real ones. Cue the meltdown: shame, fear, and a $3,000 legal bill. But here's the kicker—she was wrong. You can't trademark a hashtag. BUT... she was right about one thing: if your idea is gold, you better protect it.

At the time, it felt like the end. But life is improv, my friends. That setback forced me to rethink everything. I realized the reason people struggled with personal branding wasn't a lack of strategy—it was a lack of courage. They feared failure. Rejection. Being seen.

That realization led to the concept that became Fear Is My Homeboy.

That cease-and-desist? It wasn't the end of my story. It was the beginning of the right one. So if you're face-palming through a setback right now, remember this: life isn't trying to ruin you. It's handing you a gift.

You just might have to dig through some shit to find it.

In fields of white, the black sheep stands,
marked by fate, not by chance.
While others flock and stay the same,
she's drawn to fire, pulled by flame.

They mock her wool that's dark as night,
they scorn her steps, deny its light.
But deep inside, she feels the spark—
a quiet bite, a bigger bark.

While others graze on grassy plains,
the black sheep dreams of distant gains:
a mountain's peak, a starlit sky,
an endless climb, one wild try.

They call her odd, they call her strange,
they whisper doubt, they fear the change.
But undeterred, she finds a way
to turn her black coat into ballet.

A sheep once shunned, now ready to dance—
center stage now, there's no looking back.
Reaching heights she'd never boast,
the black sheep finally takes her place as GOAT.

For in that wool so darkly cast
was strength to prevail, to outlast.
She climbs to where most won't go—
she finds the way.

The black sheep is home.

PEOPLE PLEASING ISN'T LOVE.
IT IS FEAR.

NOT AN IMPOSTER

You are not an imposter—you are expanding. Imposter Syndrome isn't a sign that you don't belong. It's a sign that you're stepping up.

Here's the thing about fear: it throws its biggest punches right before a breakthrough. The closer you get to leveling up, the louder fear gets. Why? Because fear knows that if you cross that finish line, you evolve. You get braver. You need it less. So in a last-ditch effort to keep you "safe," fear pulls out all the stops—self-doubt, procrastination, perfectionism, and of course, Imposter Syndrome.

But here's the truth: Imposter Syndrome hasn't arrived. YOU have arrived. It means you're playing bigger. You're stretching into something new. You're expanding.

So what if, instead of seeing Imposter Syndrome as a stop sign, we saw it as a green light? A sign that we're on the edge of growth. That we're exactly where we're meant to be.

Because the people who don't feel Imposter Syndrome? They're not pushing themselves. They're not stepping into uncharted territory. They're staying the same.

So if you feel it, congratulations. You are doing it right. Now keep going, HOLLER at those dreams. And here's the bonus: research shows that people with proactive personalities—those who take action despite fear—are happier, healthier, and more fulfilled.

So next time Imposter Syndrome sneaks in, remind yourself: this isn't fear telling you to stop.

It's proof that you're ready for more.

IMPOSTER SYNDROME HASN'T ARRIVED. YOU HAVE ARRIVED. BECAUSE IF FEAR IS HERE, YOU'RE DOING IT RIGHT.

MONEY TREE

I lost a lot of momentum in my business during a season of major reinvention. I was stuck in a liminal space—no longer who I had been, but not yet who I was becoming. I couldn't confidently sell, pitch, or prospect the way I used to because I lacked focus, certainty, and clarity. And when you stop picking up the phone, the craziest thing happens—it stops ringing.

That stretch of time was financially rough. I had to rebuild the machine I had spent years creating.

At one point during that season, a small money tree sat in my office—a resilient plant with braided trunks, long believed to bring prosperity and good fortune. I had originally bought it for my husband when he went full-time as an independent contractor, hoping it would bring him luck and sales. And it did. He had a record couple of years, absolutely crushing it.

Meanwhile, I was in my office with back sweat, trying to figure out who I was and how I was gonna make payroll. Dramatic? Maybe. But my revenue streams were as dry as the desert.

Then, on the first day of a new year, I walked into my office and saw the money tree sitting on my desk. In an instant, I knew what had happened—my husband had quietly gifted it back to me, sending the same luck and love I had once given him.

And while that year kicked my ass, that money tree sat in the center of my desk, reminding me that no matter how chaotic business and life get, I have the one thing that makes me the luckiest: love.

Marriage, I've learned, is a true partnership. When one person is down, the other can be their rock. And when the script inevitably flips, you return the strength and support.

That money tree still sits in my office, reminding me daily that while money may come and go, the real luck is having someone who believes in you as you find your way back home.

Where does this come from—
this need to be seen
by you?
This longing for approval
I never used to need,
from you,
but now it brings me to my knees
when you don't give it to me—
even when I'm being
the me-est version of me.
I know I need to set myself free.
I don't want to care
what you think of me.
I really shouldn't give a sh!t
whether you think I'm legit—
or a fraud.
So why do I crave your applause?
Because if I'm really being honest,
with you,
I wouldn't trade places
with you.
I don't want your life,
or to walk in
your shoes.
So I've got to stop stressing,
second-guessing,
outsourcing my blessings—
and get back to my roots.
My bones.
And make the journey back home—
to myself.
My soul.
The inner peace only I can know.
So please—
hold my crown,
and let it be known,
I'm here to take back my throne,
because I am on my way back home.

EXPRESSION EXPERIMENTS

If you wanna stay lit, you gotta stay fit. And I'm not talking glutes—I'm talking guts. Your courage. Your conviction. Your creative fire. This is fear fitness. And the way you train? You lift the weight of discomfort. On purpose. Daily.

For over a decade, I've preached the gospel of fear experiments—small, intentional acts of discomfort that build your bravery muscle. And now? We're leveling up. Because bravery is just one piece of the puzzle. If you want to move through the world with truth and soul, you also have to build your self-expression endurance. You have to train your voice, not just your volume. These aren't just habits. They're sacred training grounds.

Welcome to Self-Expression Sunday, bayyyybeeeee.

A movement inside the Hollaverse where we make a sacred Sunday commitment to building the muscle of courage, creativity, and confidence—by sharing our art. And remember: YOU ARE THE ART. So yes, this could mean sharing your actual art—your lyrics, your poetry, you on stage, a story, anything you've made. AND it could also mean sharing your vibe, your essence, your style, what you love, how you roll—showing us who you are.

Plus, I don't know about you, but I've got so many things in drafts that I'm overthinking— and this movement is my accountability partner. It forces me to face my fears weekly and JUZZZZ DO IT ALREADY!!!!

Here's the truth: you don't get good at the thing by thinking about the thing. You get good by dating it. Want to be more creative? Date your creativity. Want deeper connection? Date your people. Want to be braver? DATE YOUR BRAVERY. Get uncomfortable regularly in order to get comfortable with discomfort. Same goes for self-expression. You've got to spend time with it. Play with it. Practice. Because the only way to get better at any art is reps—and the art of being you is no exception.

So, every week I want you to think about what you're going to share on Sundays. And when Sunday rolls around? Don't overthink it. Trust. Post. Go. This community will be in the comments to cheer you on, so make sure you tag me in your post (@judiholler) so I see them, and use the hashtag #SELFEXPRESSIONSUNDAY to join the movement.

You don't wake up brave. You build courage. Through reps. Through risk. Through rhythm. The point isn't to be perfect. The point is to get in the lab. To make a little mess. To keep showing up for your own evolution—one bold, brave move at a time.

FEAR IS PROOF OF LIVING.

INTERRUPT THE PATTERN

You are not stuck. You never have been. You never will be.

But I know—it feels real. When life isn't moving how you want it to, when the weight of self-doubt, fear, or uncertainty presses down, it can feel like you're sinking in quicksand. But that's the lie. That's the trap. Because stuck is not a state of being—it's a state of mind.

Energy is always in motion, and so are you. The only reason you feel stuck is because your thoughts are running the same script, looping the same fears, doubts, and worst-case scenarios. You are replaying the problem instead of writing the solution.

So if you want a way out, you have to interrupt the pattern. Break the cycle. Introduce something new—a new thought, a new action, a new decision.

Here's how:

- Move your body. When your mind is spiraling, force a physical shift. Take a cold shower. Go for a run. Stretch. Stand in the sun.
- Change your input. If you've been feeding your mind with negativity, flip the switch. Read something inspiring. Listen to a podcast that lifts you up.
- Do one productive thing. Clean a drawer. Write one email. Pay one bill. Prove to yourself that momentum is possible.
- Stop future-tripping. Anxiety thrives in uncertainty. Instead of asking, What if it all goes wrong? ask, What if it all goes right?
- Make one decision. You don't have to fix everything overnight. But you can take one step. Make one call. Send one message. Do one thing that moves you forward.

Because you are never stuck. You are simply in between moves.

So make one.

She is no longer giving away her power.
This is her hour. Her prime. Her time.
To exist—
Loudly.
Truly.
Finally.
Freely.
Y E T
Secretly, she insists
that she's twisted,
because something has shifted.
Just as predicted,
she's changed—again.
Fearing what others will say
as she PAVES a new way.
Trying to turn down the doubt
that now feels too loud.
So she closes her eyes—
puff puff pass
it disappears like a cloud.
She takes it all in with a—
Deep. Breath.
A N D
as predicted,
when she opens her eyes,
she remains convicted,
because she knows—
she is gifted.
A unicorn. A good witch. An anomaly.
Fully free.
Being who she was born to be—
Honestly. Solidly.
No longer a wannabe.
Living out her destiny.
Audibly asking for what she needs.
Stepping into her sovereignty.
Not afraid to be seen.
Loudly. Truly. Finally. Freely.
Hollering at her dreams.

THE COVER STORY

I have to tell you what went down with the cover of this book. I now call it the day I officially came out of the creative closet. I've always been a creative, but somewhere along the way, I lost myself. And as I began to connect the dots—through years of self-discovery—I realized one of the patterns that led me off track: when I reached a certain level of success and started making real money, the money grabbers started circling.

These are the people who sniff around your brand, your vibe, your essence. They have "ideas." Rebrand this. Fix that. Scale like this. "If you want to keep up, you've got to do what everyone else is doing." Some are well-intentioned—and yes, I've brought in voices that have helped me tremendously. But here's the thing: no outside opinion is worth outsourcing the very essence that built you. Because when you do, you hand over your power.

Case in point: the cover of this book. When it came time to finalize it, I froze. I couldn't decide. I was pacing the hallways of my head, losing sleep, snapping at people, burning time, energy, and money. Then it hit me—the reason I couldn't decide on the cover was because the title wasn't mine.

This book was originally called Be The Verb, a phrase given to me by a well-meaning brand manager who thought it would make me more marketable in corporate America. And in a moment of fear—afraid of losing my keynote business, my main revenue stream—I said yes. I changed my website. I changed the title. I gave away my power.

But here's what I now know: if something doesn't belong to you, it won't stay with you. And you won't want to stay with it.

So I shut it all down. I called my power back. I renamed this book the way I always knew it was meant to be. Holler at Your Dreams™. The cover that followed came from my soul. And sometimes, I get chills thinking about how close I came to missing this magic.

Never let someone outside of you tell you how to be you. I built myself by hollering at my dreams. Now it's your turn. So if you're giving away your power to people who don't know your path... stop it. If you're letting your brain get louder than your soul... call it back. If you're afraid to fully express because you think it'll cost you everything... remember, it might be the thing that sets you free.

Your one wildly dope soul always knows.
Trust her.

If something doesn't belong to you, it will not stay with you.

(and you won't want to stay with it)

The moment serendipity hits—
when you hear the universe for the first time—
it's unlike anything ELSE,
impossible to shake from your mind.
SO, I played a game with you,
and asked for a sign,
within minutes,
there it was,
your divine gift in real time.
A smile spread across my lips,
chills ran down my spine,
faith wrapping around my hips
at the sighting of the Divine.
A whisper.
A nudge.
A knowing—
showing me I'm on the path,
headed the right way.
So I took a deep breath
and continued on with my day,
knowing my angels were close by—
and that I'd be okay.

CHOOSE WISELY

There was a season in my life when, behind closed doors, I was basically the queen of complaining—feeling sorry for myself and throwing world-class pity parties with a guest list that included all my doubts, insecurities, and unresolved frustrations. I was ranting about all the things I didn't have or hadn't achieved yet, like it was my job. And now that I think about it, it's no wonder my actual job took a hit because… oh man, we'll get there, wait for it.

But seriously, I was stuck in this toxic cycle of whining and playing the victim, which has never really been my vibe. Yet somehow, there I was—frustrated, sad, overwhelmed, angry, and straight-up mad at the world. My husband was basically running a full-time emotional support hotline for me while I lied to the rest of the world, threw up a smile, tossed some deuces, and acted like life was all aces.

Then one day, it hit me. Like, full-on faceplant hit me: if I know what I don't want, what pisses me off, and what I'm no longer willing to tolerate, that also means I know what I do want, what makes me happy, and what I want to keep doing more of. That realization was a gut punch wrapped in a gift—it snapped me back to reality and reminded me of one undeniable truth.

And trust me, you're gonna wanna bust out your hot pink highlighter for this one:

If you can manifest what you desire, you can also manifest what you complain about.

Words are wands, yo. And that truth woke me up faster than a shot of espresso, snapping me out of my "poor me" mentality straight into "oh, try me, motherf*cker" mode. I remembered who I was—the self-made girl who earned everything she has through blood, sweat, and hot pink hustle. And I wasn't about to go down without a fight—even if that meant fighting myself to get her back.

So let this set you free: if you know what you don't want, you also know what you do. And if you can manifest what you desire, you can absolutely manifest what you complain about.

Choose wisely.

her.

What does she have that I don't?
This is what I think
as I watch her follower count grow—
like a summer storm that won't slow.

What is wrong with me?
This is what I feel
as my confidence spills away—
like a bottle unsealed.

What does she know that I don't know?
This is what I say
as I start to question my own way—
like an echo with nowhere to go.

Maybe today,

I'll put down my phone,
trust my bones,
and finally dethrone
this device
that lights up my ego—
instead of my soul.

THE CREATIVE C—BLOCK

When I started writing this book—especially in those early months when the idea was freshly hatched—I kept it to myself. I was in that deliciously sacred space of intuitive creation, mad momentum, and deep focus. It was my private dance with inspiration.

I knew I'd eventually share the news, and I did. I began speaking it into existence: I'm working on my next book. Saying it out loud sends mad signals to the universe. It creates accountability. It fuels momentum.

But here's the key: I never shared much more than that—not even with my closest homies. Why? Because I didn't want to get creatively f_ -blocked.

Yeah, I said it. It's bold. It's brash. And maybe even a little offensive. But so is someone stomping all over your sacred, not-yet-ready-to-be-critiqued ideas. Because let's be real: when your creative momentum gets shut down by outside noise? That is the real violation.

So yeah—I'm keeping the word. Because it fits. And because your dreams deserve the same kind of protection you'd give anything precious, personal, and powerful. And if you're not careful, it will happen. All it takes is one person who doesn't understand your dream to kill your momentum.

One random family member's "feedback" to make you overthink everything.
One negative comment to make you want to hide.
One coworker's "opinion" to stop you in your tracks.

It's like Dr. Dre in the studio.

Imagine him making a fire beat and then saying, "Yo, world, what do you think? Is it good enough? You guys like it?" Nah. Dre makes the beat, perfects the beat, drops the beat—then says, You're welcome.

Here's the truth: your creative beginnings are fragile.
They are sacred. They need protection.

When you're birthing something new, trust yourself enough to keep it close. Keep your head down, your heart open, and the noise out. Write daily. Trust the process. Let there be something about your work the world doesn't know yet—something still marinating in your soul.

And when it's ready? Drop the beat.

WHY YOU ARE "STUCK"

Let's be real—most people don't fail because they're not talented or capable. They stay stuck because of patterns they don't even realize they're repeating.

Here are a few of the big ones:

- Not believing in yourself
- Comparison
- Complaining
- Trying to do it all, alone
- Lack of focus
- People-pleasing
- The inability to delegate
- Uncertainty
- Overthinking
- Perfectionism
- Lack of boundaries
- Procrastination
- Living in the past
- Waiting for permission
- The fear of failure
- The fear of success

If you saw yourself in any of these, good.

That's not weakness—it's awareness.
And awareness is where momentum begins.

Instead of—
  chasing
    chasing
      chasing
DREAMS
what if you started
  making
    making
      making
DREAMS happen.
Aren't you exhausted from all that running?
Running away.
  Running toward.
    Running from.
      Running to
something outside of you—
when this whole time,
it's always been you.
WHAT IF
you let your dreams
catch up with you?
Let them grab you by the shoulders,
point straight at your soul,
look you dead in the eyes,
and say—
"Right there. That's where I want to go.
Take me there."
To which you'd say...
"Okay. Show me the way."
And then it would begin—
the first day
of being a verb.
Using your spoken word
to HOLLER at your dreams.
Sinking fear like a submarine,
no longer afraid to be seen,
confidence stealing the scene—
as you turn into a dream machine.
Crowning yourself,
the ultimate Queen.

YOU'RE LOST. LEARNING RHYTHM

NOT YOU'RE THE OF YOUR BECOMING.

GRAVEYARD OF DREAMS

One of my favorite quotes of all time is the Les Brown "graveyard of dreams" quote.

Honestly, it reads more like a piece of poetry than a quote—an epitaph, an invitation, an anthem, a power ballad, and a call to action that reminds us that success goes to those who keep moving.

Here's what he writes:

"The graveyard is the richest place on earth, because it is here that you will find all the hopes and dreams that were never fulfilled, the books that were never written, the songs that were never sung, the inventions that were never shared, the cures that were never discovered—all because someone was too afraid to take that first step, keep with the problem, or determined to carry out their dream."

Look, the world is overflowing with would-be authors, artists, musicians, dancers, and visionaries—full of bright, beautiful, innovative ideas.

The problem is that most of those epic ideas will end up in the graveyard of dreams because the doubt was louder than the dream, the fear was stronger than the faith, and the comparison more powerful than their courage.

If you want to avoid the graveyard of dreams, you have to Holler at Your Dreams. It's the only solution because you can't shake the world if you're standing still.

This is a state of emergency!
Your mind—
Divine, like a fine wine.
What gets in there
can break you or make you.
Your brain—
Did you know?
It processes 60,000 thoughts a day. Science, yo.
And 80% of them are negative,
which feels like a good incentive
to be preventative
of the expletives
that feel decorative—
but are actually wrecking us.

                                                          This is a state of emergency!
                                                                               Your body—
                                                             a temple, a vessel,
                                   carrying you from place to place,
                                            day to day, year to year.
                                                            Your heart—
                                                             Did you know?
                                 It beats 100,000 times a day.
                     That's 35 million beats a year. Science, yo.
             So maybe we should stop taking it for granted—
                                        this engine that chants,
                                   a million beats on demand,
                                       with no other plans than
                     to keep the rhythm while we expand.

This is a state of emergency!
Your soul—
it always knows, deep in your bones,
if it's a yes or it's a no.
But your ego? It loves control.
Did you know—
Ego is just identity in a role, built on fear,
doubt, and self-patrol. Science, yo.
It'll trick your mind, get you misaligned,
have you thinking
you're better than— or less than.
But you are neither. You are the ether.
You are the breath
between lightning and thunder.
You are like no other—different by design,
divinely by wonder.

DUCT TAPE

My dad used to drive this old wood-paneled station wagon. My 80s/90s kids will know the one—the kind with the extra backseat that faced the wrong way, zero seatbelts. (That era was unhinged, and I love it. Shoutout to my Gen X peeps!) My siblings and I would fight like Vikings over that prized seat so we could wave at cars behind us or get truckers to honk. Looking back, it was a vibe. But at the time? I was mortified.

Especially because my dad—resourceful and practical as hell—fixed everything on that car with duct tape. Loose paneling? Duct tape. Something rattling? Duct tape. "Duct tape'll fix just about anything," he'd say. And now, all these years later, I can't see a roll without thinking of him. But back then, I didn't think it was charming. I thought it was embarrassing.

We didn't have much. And to attend the all-girls Catholic high school I had my heart set on, I had to help make it happen. I worked all through high school—at restaurants, giving my parents the money to help cover tuition. I was also part of the school's work-study program, which meant I got discounted tuition in exchange for painting in the summers and cleaning, organizing, or emptying trash during the year. I used to hide from my friends when I was assigned odd jobs during school hours. Only about 10-15% of us were on work-study, and I was so ashamed.

As if that weren't enough, every morning my dad would drive me to school in that duct-taped station wagon. And every morning, I'd lie and ask him to drop me off down the street. I told him my classes started in the back building. They didn't. But I couldn't bear the thought of pulling up next to the girls in their cherry-red Jeep Wranglers or spotless white Suzuki Sidekicks in our patched-up ride. And my sweet dad... he knew. He always knew. And he never said a word.

I look back on that time now with tears in my eyes—not from shame, but from pride. Because yo, that duct tape held a lot more than that station wagon together. It held me together.

I didn't realize it then, but that season planted every seed of who I am now.

I was exposed to a level of excellence and elegance I'd never known. I saw what was possible. I learned how to work. I learned how to contribute. I learned that presence matters more than privilege. That resourcefulness is a superpower. That grace and grit can coexist. I learned how to talk to people, how to manage time, how to organize a system, how to lead.

I was duct-taping my life together, but I was also building a ladder out of the environment I was born into—and toward the life I dreamed about.

I was expanding. Reaching. Stepping into rooms that would pull me toward a different future. And while I was embarrassed then, I am so damn grateful now. Because duct tape gets a bad rap. But sometimes? Duct tape is divine. It's not a weakness. It's a witness. Proof that you're still trying. Still showing up. Still finding a way.

So if you're holding it together with metaphorical duct tape right now—don't apologize. It's not something to hide. It's something to honor.

That chip on my shoulder,
she's a diligent soldier,
a fierce controller,
a bitter upholder,
making me colder.
heavy like a boulder,
I can no longer hold her,
so I set her down,
feeling a little bit bolder,
as I let my future unfold her.

He tells me to enjoy the slow time,
because it won't last for a long time,
so I might as well have a good time—
am I right?
He says,
Slow down.
Get a massage.
Write.
Move.
And deep down,
I know he's right.
So maybe—just maybe—
I'll finally listen this time,
because what do I have to lose,
besides my mind...
and more
time.

IT ENDS WITH ME

Some people build an entire identity around the things that didn't go their way. The heartbreak. The hardship. The betrayal. The absence. The loss. They wear it like a badge, a brand, a storyline they never stop telling.

But here's the dangerous truth: when you worship the wound, you stay wounded. You start to believe your pain is your personality. That your past is your ceiling. That you'll never be more than what happened to you. But pain isn't meant to be your prison—it's meant to be your portal.

For a long time, I thought life was unfair. Especially when it came to relationships with certain family members. I didn't have the support system other people seemed to have. And for years, I let that hurt hold the pen.

But eventually, I made a decision. A new mantra emerged: Break the cycle.

There's a quote I once read that stopped me cold: "It ran in my family until it ran into me." I don't know who said it, but it became my battle cry.

I decided my wounds would make me a warrior. A soldier for setting myself free. I stopped worshipping what went wrong and started honoring what could go right. That pain became my power. It showed me who I didn't want to be—and that clarity became my anchor. It's why I am who I am today.

Yes, your pain shaped you. But it doesn't define you. Yes, it matters. But it doesn't get to rule you. Yes, it happened. But it's not happening anymore—unless you keep inviting it in.

Worshipping the wound is worshipping the problem. You can't create the life you want while bowing to the thing that broke you. You can't holler at your dreams while staying loyal to the bitterness. You can't claim your future while clinging to what was.

Let the wound heal. Let it run into you.

Life hands her no script,
no playbook,
no first look.
So instead of predictions,
what if she stayed convicted—
Devoted,
Re-coded,
to H O P E.
Letting in what fuels her soul.
(which only she knows)
Wouldn't that be dope?

IDENTITY CRISIS

This book wouldn't exist if I hadn't lost myself.

And I'm not talking about a cute "I took a sabbatical to rediscover my joy" kind of lost. I'm talking about full-on confusion. Sadness. Isolation. Anger. The kind of dark night of the soul that strips you of everything you thought you were—and leaves you staring at the mess, wondering what's left.

I've said it more than once: if you met me between 2022 and 2024, you didn't really meet me. I was so disoriented. I was afraid of my own shadow. Everything I had built was shifting. What used to work stopped working. I couldn't see what was next, and I had no idea who I was becoming.

But now I know: that confusion wasn't a failure—it was a doorway. Because sometimes, you have to lose yourself to find yourself. You hit an edge—emotionally, spiritually, professionally—and everything in you starts asking, Is this it? That question feels terrifying. But it's also the spark. It's the moment of divergence. The initiation into the next version of you.

And if you're feeling that now—let me tell you something: you're not broken. You're becoming. I swear, this book, this movement, this mission—none of it would've been born if I hadn't been cracked open. That identity crisis saved me. It made space for the real one. Not Corporate Barbie Judi. Not good-girl-performing Judi. The one I was always meant to be.

Because when you hit a personal rock bottom, you realize something beautiful: you've got nothing to lose. So you might as well rebuild it exactly how you want it. I did. I cleaned out my circle. Rebuilt my team. Reimagined my voice. I chose to create a life, a business, and an art form that matched the soul I had finally uncovered.

And if I can do that—you can too.

So if you're confused? If you feel like nothing fits anymore? Good. You're right on time. Reinvention doesn't begin with clarity. It begins with loss. With doubt. With holy discomfort. Let it break you open. Let it reroute your entire life. Because the real you isn't behind you. She's on the other side of this moment—waiting to be met.

We've decided to go another direction.
It's not you.
It's us.
Really.
Truly.
But thank you.
Maybe next time.
OK, I'm not fine—.
They say it's just redirection,
all this rejection,
protection.
So why does it hurt?
Make me question my worth?
All of this dirt
is messing with my vibe.
I can't help but feel
like I'm running out of time.
I used to be so good at trusting my life—
but now I just feel like I'm losing my mind,
having to swallow my pride,
as I reach deep down inside
to pull out the light—
and Holler at these Dreams of mine
with faith,
not fight.

R.B.F.

I was on stage in Dallas, fully in the zone, delivering what I thought was an epic talk—until I locked eyes with her. If you've heard of RBF (resting b*tch face), this woman had it. And the second I saw her, she slayed me with it. She loathed me. I just knew it. Despised me. I was convinced she was about to drag me off stage Showtime at the Apollo style. I. Was. Shook. I tried to ignore her, but my eyes kept finding hers. And from that moment on, I stopped speaking to the audience—I started performing for her, desperate to change her mind. I let my own thoughts hijack my joy. No one else knew... but I knew. And that's enough to ruin the vibe.

After the talk, I pulled myself together for the book signing. The line was long, but early on, the vibes were high. Two women ran up to me—first in line—gushing over how much they loved me and my talk. We snapped selfies, hugged, and my ego was living for this moment with my new fangirl besties. (More on them in just a minute.) And as my ego was basking in their praise, I saw her. RBF. In line. Oh God. What does she want? Roast me in front of everyone? Chuck a book at my head?

I braced myself. She stepped up, grabbed my shoulders, and with tears in her eyes, said, "You have no idea how timely your talk was for me today. I lost my son, Joseph, a year ago this week. I've been afraid to be happy. Your words reminded me I have to stop fearing what I can't control—and set myself free. I need to be Joseph's mom, not just someone who lost a son. From this day forward, that is how I will honor him." Whoa. She wasn't judging me on stage—she was processing. Feeling. Transforming. We hugged. Snapped a selfie. She walked away.

Then I hit the restroom before heading to the airport. That's when I heard them—my two fangirls—except this time, they weren't fangirling. They were trash-talking me, assuming I'd already left. I wish I could tell you I walked out of the stall and shut them down. I didn't. I morphed right back into grade-school Judi—hiding in the stall, pulling my feet up until they left. I stayed there for ten minutes. Shaking. Sweating. Mortified. Pissed. And—grateful. Because God handed me a big one that day: never trust a frown—or a smile.

You never know what someone's carrying. The only thing you can control is how you show up. Are you leading with love? Are you being yourself? Are you having fun? Do you love yourself? That moment taught me to stop judging my audiences. You don't need to perform for the faces—you need to trust your voice. And for the record: no one sits through a keynote grinning like Barney for an hour.

And RBF? For me, it now stands for: Really Big Feels. A reminder to breathe, trust the moment, and never stop being you.

False Gods.
Poser prophets.
We worship so much
outside of us—
idolizing people,
followers,
likes,
and fans.
Bowing down to houses,
bags,
shoes,
and brands.
Obsessed with other people's
prized possessions,
we disconnect from the real lessons—
the ones serving up the only blessings
that truly matter.
Like—
self-expression.
Love.
Faith.
Hope.
Courage.
Kindness.
And above all—
growth.

SOMEDAY SYNDROME

One of my best friends lost her mom to Alzheimer's when her mom was barely in her 60s. My friend is an only child—her mom was her best friend. Her dad, a successful CEO and businessman, had spent nearly 40 years building a beautiful life for their family. Together, they dreamed of their retirement—their "someday"—when they would travel the world and see all the places they'd always talked about. Italy, Greece, the Amalfi Coast, Ireland—all of it. They had a whole bucket list planned and were ready to do it right once retirement hit.

But they never made it. They didn't get to do any of it.

Her mom was diagnosed with Alzheimer's long before they ever got the chance to board a plane. While her dad worked his whole life to build the future they dreamed of, time slipped away. Instead of exploring Europe, he found himself caring for his wife as her memory faded. All those big plans they put on pause for "someday" never came to life.

Because that's the thing: Someday Syndrome will slowly steal your future one grain of sand at a time.

While we make plans and talk about the future like it's guaranteed, the truth is, anything can happen. You can have the most rock-solid retirement plan, a killer 401(k), and your entire bucket list mapped out—but nothing in this life is promised. That doesn't mean we don't plan for the future or act recklessly—but it does mean we have to start seeing today as the special occasion it already is.

So why do we wait for a "someday" that may never come to do all our favorite things? Why do we save the things we love for later, when later might never arrive?

Today is the special occasion.

Wear your favorite outfit.
Spray the expensive perfume.
Use the china.
Drink the good wine.
Light the fancy candle.
Eat the cupcake.

These are the good old days. You're living them right now, so you might as well enjoy the show—because today is the youngest you will ever be.

I'll never take my comfort
for granted again.
Even when the plan
doesn't go as I planned it—
God's plan is the anthem.
And the moment you trust it,
you unhand it.

HEY JEALOUSY

Jealousy isn't just an ugly feeling—it's an invitation from your future self. When you feel that sting, that twist in your gut while scrolling or watching someone else shine, it's not because you don't like them. It's because something in them is mirroring a version of you that you're too afraid to express.

Jealousy is data. A mirror. A reflection of your own unlived potential. It shows you what you want—but haven't yet claimed. And here's the wild part: science shows that jealousy actually activates the same neural pathways as physical pain. It literally hurts. But that pain isn't punishment—it's guidance. And studies say we feel it most when we see someone like us succeed. Which means your jealousy isn't proof you're behind. It's proof you're close.

Usually, the only difference between you and the person you envy is this: one of you is self-expressing, the other isn't. One is posting, pitching, showing up, willing to look cringe. The other is waiting, overthinking, worrying what people will think. One is playing. One is pausing. And while they're getting richer, bolder, more magnetic—you're just getting more resentful.

I've been there. Jealous of the prettier woman, the busier speaker, the one who had what looked like it all. But I didn't hate her. I hated how I was hiding. So I stopped hating—and started studying. I turned jealousy into research.

It's incredibly important to understand that jealousy ranks dangerously low on the emotional guidance scale—below anger, below rage, and just a few steps above grief and despair. It will block your blessings, bankrupt your confidence, and poison your pace. So now, when I feel it, I interrupt the spiral with: "Good for her. If she can, I can."

Then I ask: What is this showing me about where I want to grow?

That's how you take your power back.
That's how you flip jealousy into jet fuel.

I am tired.
So tired.
Of my own bullshit.
Of beating myself up.
Of the worry, the fear, the anxiety—
Of what will be,
And will I be—
Enough this time?
Or am I past my prime?
The constant loops in my mind
have me wondering, for the first time,
if I'd be better off not alive.
Yeah. You read that right.
It was just a flash,
but damn, it scared my ass.
Thank goodness it passed,
but it put my focus on blast—
had me ask:
What am I really running from?
Myself?
Rejection?
Failure?
Stress?
Maybe it's success—
or the need to impress—
that has me second-guessing all of it.
Running from all of it,
Fearing all of it,
Blocking all of it.
So maybe,
it's time to stop running.
Maybe it's time to sit down,
unlace my shoes,
kick them off,
do what I know I need to do—
slow down
so I can hear
what's been calling me
all along.

THE COST OF STAYING

We've all stayed too long. In the wrong friendship. The wrong relationship. The wrong job. The wrong group chat. Not because we didn't know better, but because we were afraid to do better. There's that famous Maya Angelou quote: "When you know better, you do better." And while I love that—there's a part we don't talk about enough: doing better requires doing. You actually have to make a move. You have to holler at what you need.

Leaving the wrong room doesn't happen overnight. But staying in it? That has a cost—and most of us are silently paying for it every day.

Here's what inaction steals from you:
- Your originality. You start to shrink, shapeshift, and water yourself down to fit the energy of people who never really saw you in the first place.
- Your confidence. Every time you don't speak up, every time you tolerate disrespect or dullness, you teach yourself that your voice doesn't matter.
- Your time. Which, by the way, is the one resource you never get back.
- Your joy. You start confusing comfort with peace. They're not the same.
- Your intuition. It gets drowned out by people-pleasing and fake belonging.
- Your legacy. You can't build your life if you're too busy surviving someone else's.

Signs you're in the wrong room?
- You feel drained, not energized, when you leave.
- You constantly shrink or mask parts of yourself.
- You're celebrated for who you used to be—not who you're becoming.
- Your ideas aren't valued—or worse, they're stolen.
- You find yourself gossiping, numbing, or spiraling more often than creating.

So, how do you leave the room (without losing yourself)?
- You name the truth. You don't have to burn it down. But you do have to stop pretending it's working.
- You get curious. What would a better room feel like? Who's in it? What are they creating?
- You make micro moves. You don't need a dramatic exit. You need consistent action. Start saying no more. Start showing up elsewhere.
- You protect your peace. Not everyone deserves access to your magic.
- You invest in rooms that light you up. This might mean joining a new mastermind, hiring a coach, going to a live event, or simply unfollowing the noise.

Trust and believe, leaving the wrong room is one of the most self-expressed decisions you can make.

If you want to shift dimensions,
you've got to pay attention.
Because the lesson?
It's more than pen and paper—
it's the reason your maker
made you greater.
But we say, "I'll get to that later,"
which, let's be real,
is a crime of time.
Because before you know it,
you'll be past your prime,
wishing you had more time—
when today
is the youngest you'll ever be.
So it seems to me,
today
might just be
a good day
to turn
Fear... into faith.
Doubt... into dreams.
Comfort... into courage.
Resistance... into results.
Because what makes you great
isn't the money in your bank—
it's the internal earthquake.
The guts to make instead of break.
To be a verb.
To motivate.

21

I know you've seen the ads, books, and courses that promise things like: 21 days to famous. 21 days to financial freedom. 21 days to be published. 21 days to confidence. 21 days to more sales. 21 days to becoming a completely toned size 4 with zero wrinkles. Okay, that last one is a bit dramatic, but you get the point.

There is no quick fix. No magic potion (well, maybe Botox—it's pretty close). No secret formula. No Prince Charming coming to save you. There is only focus and hard work, done consistently over time.

But here's a game-changer: 21 seconds can change your life: Forget 21 days. That's too long to wait. You can change your life, your business, your relationships, and your energy in just 21 seconds. Every micro-choice you make stacks up—just like compound interest.

It takes 21 seconds to say no.
It takes 21 seconds to say yes.
It takes 21 seconds to send the email.
It takes 21 seconds to pick up the phone.
It takes 21 seconds to smile at a stranger.
It takes 21 seconds to ask for help.
It takes 21 seconds to walk away.
It takes 21 seconds to walk in.

I've quit many things—smoking, drinking (for almost a year), skipping workouts—and while 21 days was a milestone, the real work happened in 21-second decisions. It took 21 seconds to say no to the cigarette. It took 21 seconds to say no to the drink. It took 21 seconds to grab my keys and get in the car for the gym. Stay focused. Work hard. Keep showing up. That's the only algorithm you need.

This week, notice the micro-choices you make every minute of every day. And to help, here are some simple exercises to build your 21-second muscle:

1. The 21-Second Challenge – Pick a habit you want to build and commit to doing it for 21 seconds daily. Example: make your bed, say a prayer, drink a glass of water.
2. The One-Thing Exercise – Write down one goal you want to hit. Break it into small, manageable steps, and take immediate action on the first one.
3. The 21-Second Timer – Set a 50-minute timer to work on one task without distraction. When time's up, stand up, shake out your energy for 21 seconds, then reset.
4. Small Wins Strategy – Track one small win per day in your planner. Momentum builds through micro-successes.

Remember: there's no quick fix—only hard work, done consistently, 21 seconds at a time.

Have we become so obsessed
with
the algorithm
That we've lost
our own?
Are we so busy looking around,
that we've stopped
looking inside
our soul?
Maybe it's time
to put down the phone
and pick up our lives.
Focus on what feels right
instead of trends
that will pass in the night.
Because how can you take flight
into a new dimension
when you've lost your own expression?

ON PURPOSE

God makes us uncomfortable on purpose. Because if everything stayed easy and breezy, we'd never move. We'd never stretch. We'd never grow. Comfort is cozy—and that's why we cling to it. But discomfort? That's divine disruption. That's the nudge. The invitation. The signal that it's time to evolve.

When things started falling apart for me in 2022, I got mad. Like, bitter and spiraling mad. Doors that once flew open slammed shut. Revenue streams dried up. My message felt stale. I watched others "crushing it" while I sat there feeling crushed.

And beneath it all? A rising resentment that said, Why not me? But I see now—that frustration was the point.

Because I was supposed to move. I was supposed to become someone new. And I wasn't listening. God will teach you the same lesson over and over until you do.

The discomfort wasn't punishment—it was direction. A holy disruption to push me toward something more aligned, more honest, more me. I had to rethink my message. My revenue. My rhythm. My future. I had to strip it all down to the studs and rebuild a life and business that fit the woman I was becoming. And once I finally accepted the assignment, everything unlocked.

That's the thing about pain—it's often just clarity in disguise.

So if things are shifting around you, if doors are closing and stuff's getting weird, don't panic. Pay attention. You might be standing at the edge of your next era.

There is no Oz. No great wizard behind the curtain with your answers. The call is coming from inside the house. You already have the shoes. So take a breath, click your heels, and start walking.

You're not being punished. You're being positioned.
On purpose.

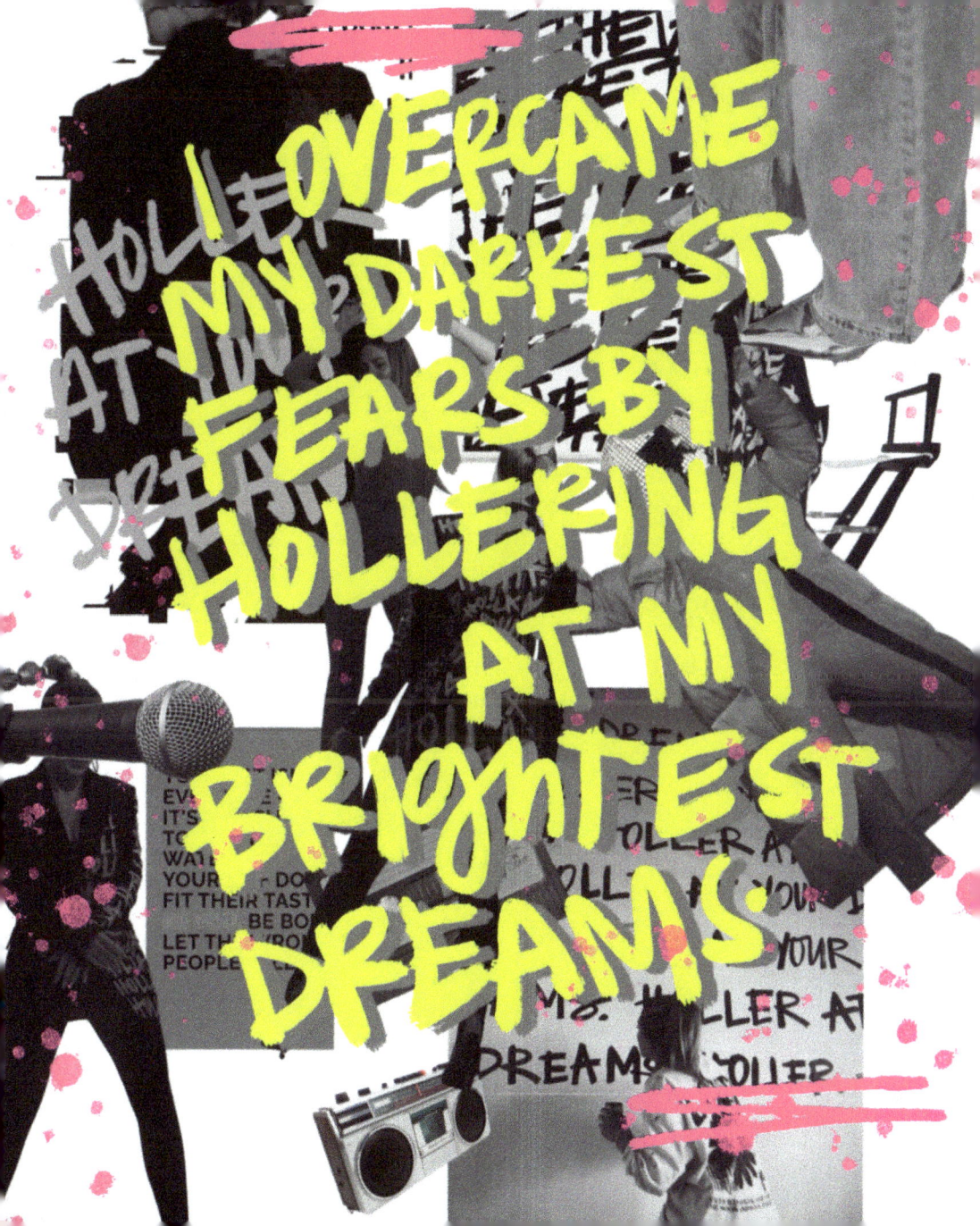

You knew.
Long before she showed her hand.
You knew.
You wanted it to be real — not leverage.
But you knew.
Let that be the last time
you don't listen to your gut the first time.

AFTER THE FALL

One of the biggest blocks to our dreams is the fear of failure. The fear of rejection. The fear of getting it wrong in public. Of being embarrassed. Judged. Canceled. Laughed at. Ignored. So we don't holler at our dreams. We overthink them. We shrink them. We bury them before they ever get a chance to breathe.

And yet, rejection and failure are the very proof that you're in the arena. That you're doing it right. If you've been rejected, failed, flopped, or fallen lately—congratulations. I'm proud of you. Because that means you showed up.

As self-expressionists, we don't aim for perfection. We aim for momentum. We don't worship the win—we honor the lesson. We treat life like a laboratory, and every mistake is data. Every rejection is redirection. Every failure is a future story. There's a phrase from improv that gets said in our house all the time: "No mistakes, only gifts." You either win or you learn—but you never lose.

And here's the part most people forget: you're in practice. Just like doctors practice medicine. Just like athletes practice free throws. Just like chefs practice technique, or musicians practice their scales, or actors rehearse their lines. I always say I have a speaking practice—because every time I step on stage, I get sharper, braver, bolder.

It's not about being flawless. It's about being in practice—and practicing is how we become iconic.

Still, when you're in it, reclaiming your power can feel impossible. So here's how you begin:

- Feel it. Don't bypass the pain. Move through it honestly. Write it out. Cry it out. Say it out loud.
- Zoom out. You're not being punished. You're being prepared. Ask: what is this teaching me?
- Reframe it. Instead of "I failed," try "I experimented." Instead of "I was rejected," try "I was redirected."
- Collect the data. What worked? What didn't? What would I try differently next time?
- Get back in the lab. Create something. Anything. Movement restores power. Don't freeze. Flow.

Your power doesn't disappear when you fail—it just hides in the wreckage. The most powerful people don't chase perfection. They chase momentum.

She runs from pain
to pleasure.
Only when she gets there,
she's surprised to find more pain.
Because wherever she goes —
there she is.
She can't outrun her pain.
She can't hide from her reflection.
She can't hustle her way to healing.
The answer she seeks
isn't in the spotlight,
the scroll,
or the next big thing.
it lives in her silence.
Her breath.
Her ache.
Her now.

PANTYHOSE PTSD

I built my career in corporate America—in the hotel industry. An industry that built me: I learned professionalism, poise, and the power of being prepared. But I also learned how to play small in heels. Back then, the dress code was a silent contract. You wore the Limited (iykyk) suit. You slid into your Ann Taylor pumps. You tugged on the pantyhose without complaint. It was the uniform. The standard. So when I left corporate and stepped into entrepreneurship, I thought I was free. But surprise: I had pantyhose PTSD.

That same instinct to conform, to be "appropriate," to never stand out too much—came with me. I was building a brand, but I was still dressing and delivering like I was about to give a site visit instead of a keynote. I had these unspoken rules stitched into my psyche, whispering things like: Keep it polished. Don't scare them off. Just blend in, Holler.

But slowly, that started to shift. First it was jeans and a blazer. Then hot pink. Then full-blown sequin suits. Not as a costume or a mask—but as an intentional practice. Because if I was out there talking about courage, fear, and authenticity, I had to embody it. And yo, nothing wakes up a ballroom faster than a woman in head-to-toe sequins before breakfast.

I mean, just imagine me walking through the lobby at 7 AM by myself, flexing my courage muscle with every step. That was the point. Every time I wore something hot pink or covered in sequins, I was in the laboratory—experimenting with my fear, building my courage muscle. And while sometimes I got high-fives and head nods and smiles from other wildly dope souls, I also got snickers, sneers, and double takes—enough to make your heart race. But I din't care, I was on a mission and walking the talk, quite literally.

Today, my keynote wardrobe includes graffiti-covered suits—custom art with my message literally woven into the fabric. What started as a style evolution became a full expression revolution. Because this isn't about the pantyhose. It's about the programming—the conditioning that can be hard to break out of. Sometimes the hardest thing to shake off is the belief that you have to look like or be like everyone else to be taken seriously. True self-expression isn't about masking or performing or hiding behind a costume. It's about remembering that you are the art. And whatever full expression of that art you decide to share with the world—as long as it comes from your soul—it's already the right choice.

I always say, if you don't look back at the earliest expressions of yourself and feel a little bit embarrassed, then you probably waited too long. I look back at the early expressions of myself—sequins and all, bad outfits and all, bad hair and all—and I'm proud of her. Because she was moving. She was expressing. She was becoming. And all of that expression helped her find her way back home to herself. And I will continue to evolve—because every decade, every year, every day, I change. And so do you.

Sometimes, the hardest thing to take off is the belief that you have to fit in or conform. And you will be tempted to do what everyone else is doing.

Don't.

If only…
regret never lingered,
second chances lasted forever,
and there was no such thing as a last dance.

If only…
days stretched longer,
dogs lived as long as we do,
and ice cream didn't melt so soon.

If only…
hate was erased,
anger faded like echoes,
and love was all that remained.

If only…
youth was infinite,
aging was effortless,
we had more time.

BIG BUT'S

But I'm too old.
But I'm not married.
But I have bills to pay.
But I don't know what I'm doing.
But I don't have a degree.
But I'm not retired yet.
But I have kids.
But I don't have kids.
But what if someone doesn't like it?
But what if I make a mistake?
But I don't have the money.
But I don't have the time.

Sound familiar?

Listen, I like big butts and I cannot lie (pun fully intended).

But Sir Mix-a-Lot aside, these kinds of but's? Nah. These are the bad, dangerous but's—the ones that definitely don't look cute in jeans and only keep you from your dreams.

We need to avoid these but's at all costs because they're basically a list of excuses hiding behind bad habits. They keep you stuck. Safe. And just the same.

At some point, you have to ignore the but's and make a move.

WHILE OTHERS WERE GETTING RICH OFF MY INSECURITIES I WAS GOING SOUL BANKRUPT.

3 SECONDS OF COURAGE

Last week, I was sitting in a sunny Scottsdale meeting room with about two dozen female founders. We had gathered around a beautifully crafted wooden farm table, sipping freshly brewed iced teas, sharing ideas, and troubleshooting challenges. At one point, a powerful question was posed: "What am I not taking action on in my business because I'm afraid?"

An epic discussion ensued. Honest admissions started flowing:

I'm not showing my face on social because what if I embarrass myself?
I don't make sales calls because what if they say no?
I haven't hired my first team member because what if I can't afford it?
I hold back from sharing what I know because what if it means less for me?
I don't set boundaries because what if I upset someone else?

On and on it went.

I don't do "x" (the thing that would grow my business) because "x" (the fear that's holding me back).

But hold up—what if it went right?

What if showing up as yourself inspires someone else?
What if that sales call books business?
What if hiring a rockstar makes you more money?
What if sharing what you know grows your following?
What if setting boundaries reduces overwhelm?

Sometimes, all it takes is three seconds of courage to change your life.
Three. Seconds.

Hitting "post" on social takes three seconds.
Picking up the phone takes three seconds.
Asking for help takes three seconds.
Sharing a hot tip takes three seconds.
Saying "no" takes three seconds.

Bravery doesn't have to be big. It's the small, everyday brave moves that become your competitive edge.

A hundred pieces of broken glass
A hundred pieces of broken glass
A disco ball is nothing more
than hundreds of shattered shards of glass.
But if you ask me what I see,
it's certainly
N O T
a hundred pieces of broken glass.
I see hope
I see light
I see brilliance
I see might
I see a mess that became magic.
And honestly?
Not having it would be tragic.
So I wonder—
What if:
All the pain is actually power?
All the dirt grows us into a flower?
If fear is actually a door?
What if this whole time, we were made for even more?
I see hope
I see light
I see brilliance
I see might
I see anything at all—
because in the end
we are all mirror balls.

SPARKS

Spark sound:
The bass drop—its vibration rattling my bones from head to toe, waking up the deepest parts of my soul, making me feel whole as I let the beat take me home.

Spark smell:
Breakfast! Is there anything better? I instantly think of my dad and life at home on Tortosa Road, as he filled the house with the smells of love—bacon and eggs, pancakes with OJ—starting our day the Mike Holler way.

Spark taste:
Coffee, first thing in the morning—the bitter, beautiful kiss hitting my lips. Not just waking up my sleepy cells, but taking me home to the quiet place I go just minutes before the world takes control.

Spark touch:
The crack of a new book opening. Feeling the spine. Peeling back the cover. Flipping through the pages with anticipation—because each story I read plants a seed.

Spark sight:
A hummingbird sipping sweet nectar from a desert tree. Reminding me, as I smile, that my real job is to be a hummingbird—confidently moving from flower to flower, finding my power in the variety of life and all its endless possibilities.

Footnote:
In 2022, I turned to The Spark Journal by the poet, Atticus, to help me use my creativity to move through a lot of pain. So, snaps to Atticus and a shoutout to the journal—if you're looking for a creative spark, it's a beautiful place to start.

Maybe today,
instead of anxious,
I'll be a blank canvas—
open to receiving,
deeply believing,
confidently weaving
all my
colors
together,
so I can courageously conceive
what's meant for me.
Because that's what the world really needs—
more people out there,
Hollering at their dreams.

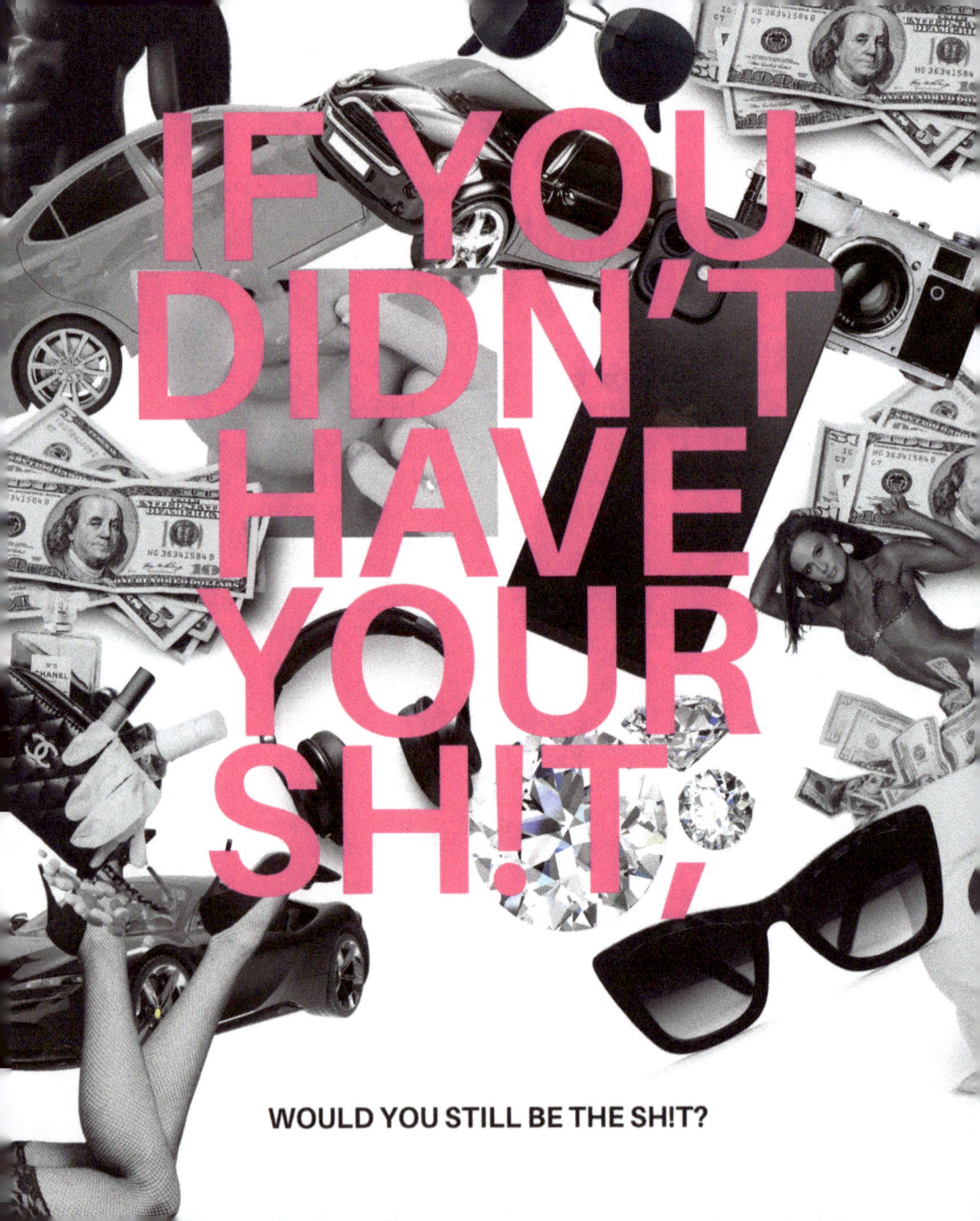

When I walked into my first slam poetry show, I had no idea that a T-shirt on the wall—"Poetry is cheaper than therapy" would hit me like a bomb of clarity. Because on these slam stages, we work sh!t out.

Tough sh!t.
  Hard sh!t.
    Real sh!t.
      Raw sh!t.

And we're all carrying sh!t.

Different sh!t.
  Inspiring sh!t.
    Brave sh!t.
      Bold sh!t.

One of my favorite things about slamming? Stepping up to the mic, about to spit something sic, and saying, "New sh!t." To let the audience know it's a new piece of art is being born, to which the audience responds right back with: "New sh!t!" to let you know they got you. It's a ritual. A sh!t exchange, if you will. Like: I'm about to do some new sh!t, and you're going to lovingly listen.

Wait… does that mean you're eating sh!t? Okay, sorry. I digress. But here we are—in the middle of a sh!t sandwich. Together. In community. Working it out. Because look…

Pain only turns into power when it has somewhere to go.
Darkness only becomes light when you flip the switch.
Suffering only turns into wisdom when it's met with gratitude.
Storms only pass when the wind dies down.
And sh!t only becomes fertilizer when you let it out.

Look. You can't hide from your inner sh!t. You can't eat it away. Numb it away. Buy it away. Wish it away. Complain it away. Exercise it away.

You have to face it and proudly declare: Sh!t, I see you. You stink. You embarrass me. I don't like you. But damn, I need you.

So, I'm planting you in my garden. Because dirt grows us into flowers. And flowers? They need fertilizer to thrive. So let's GROW. Let's bloom. Let's build a botanical garden of badassery up in this mo fo. One that stands the sh!tstorm of time.

Wait—could this poem win a world record for the most sh!ts said in a slam? Or is this just the sh!ttiest poem I've ever written? Either way, it's a win. Because sh!t? It makes The best fertilizer.

(fun fact: I advanced to the top 3 of a live poetry slam with this one!)

EASY LIKE E

What if I could just let it be easy?

Easy like the breeze.
    Easy like a Sunday.
        Easy like E.

See, most of my life, I've been a control freak—a habit I built, brick by brick, to survive the chaos of an unhealed mother. A defense mechanism. A shield. A way to create order in a world that felt anything but. But now, as a grown-ass woman, it gets me into trouble. And while I like a little trouble from time to time, I want the right kinda trouble, ya know? Not the kind with a capital T—the kind you bring on yourself because you've got jacked-up expectations that only lead to disappointment from trying to micromanage every moment.

Maybe Janet—Miss Jackson, if you're nasty—had it right all along. This is really a story about control. See, control freaks like me? We hate the easy button. Because easy means taking your foot off the gas. And if your foot is off the gas, you could stop moving. Or worse—crash. So we gun it. Pedal down. Ease right back into the comfort of control. Because God forbid we finish last.

And this? This is where the aha moment steps on stage, grabs the mic from me, and spits the truth: every mistake, failure, and major outtake? They all point back to control. Me trying to micromanage every moment. But when I look back at my wins—my major gains—they all happened in full-blown FLOW. Me, moving to the rhythm of my own life. Doing what felt right, instead of what felt safe. Caring more about my own opinion than the opinions of others. Finally becoming my own mother. Respecting my shit instead of expecting shit. Loving myself instead of lessening myself.

Yo, the sun doesn't stop shining because someone else thinks it's too bright. So why the f*ck should I have to dim my light? Self-love means I never have to bow down or need a king—because I am my own king, queen, joker, jester, and everything in between. I kiss my own ring, no longer afraid to be seen. Standing on soapboxes, telling my own story. No longer using someone else's wings to fly. Finally standing strong in my full glory.

So now? I'm learning to take my foot off the gas. Loosen my death grip on certainty. Let my beast out of the cage. Feel my rage—then turn it into the most beautiful pages I have yet to write. Pages that turn my darkest nights into the most beautiful sunrise. Because last time I checked, the sun doesn't dim its light just because someone else thinks it's too bright.

So, yeah... I guess this is really a story about control. About shining bright even on the days it feels like a fight. And letting life be easy.

Easy like Sunday.
    Easy like the breeze.
        Easy like E.

In the silence,
He is working.

In the uncertainty,
He is working.

In the worry,
He is working.

In the fear,
He is working.

In the delay,
He is working.

In the anxiety,
He is working.

In the liminal space,
He is working.

In the discomfort,
He is working.

In the tension,
He is working.

In the confusion,
He is working.

In the resistance,
He is working.

In the failure,
He is working.

I'm smiling outside,
but it feels like I'm dying inside.
My demons are close.
I hear them knocking at the door.
They want to come in—
ready to begin
their reckless parade of pain
that runs around my brain:
Fear.
Doubt.
Worry.
AND—
anxiety in varieties
wrapped up like a mixtape from the 90's
I need to unwind,
but I seem to be stuck in rewind
as I try to rewire
my mind—
so I can get back
to living my life,
closing one damaged door
at a time.

SO WHAT HAPPENED WAS

I gave away my power.
I trusted the wrong people.
I stopped trusting myself.
I got scared of my own shadow.
I asked for too much feedback.
I gave my light to people who didn't deserve it.
I tried to buy my way back.
I spent more than I saved—energetically and financially.
I went soul bankrupt.
I became obsessed with the algorithm.
I felt safer scrolling than facing the potential I was wasting.
I let other people's opinions be louder than my own.
I listened to my head more than my heart.
I didn't give my intuition the attention it deserves.
I felt sorry for myself.
I was bitter.
I was blocking my blessings.
I thought the people I hired were my friends.
I let people put me in a box.
I let cancel culture take me down.
I no longer felt safe to be seen.
I played it way too safe.
I wasted so much time.
I listened to the wrong people.
I avoided hard conversations.
I numbed instead of dealing.
I hustled instead of healed.
I was caught up in analysis paralysis.
I lost momentum.
I lost motivation.
I lost my mojo.
I lost myself.

I had nothing left to lose, so I let go.
I surrendered.

And that's when peace found me.

THE PEACE

"DEARLY BELOVED WE ARE GATHERED HERE TODAY TO GET THROUGH THIS THING CALLED LIFE."
PRINCE

(ACCEPT IT)

Peace isn't the absence of struggle; it's the presence of trust. It's what happens when we stop fighting what is and start working with it. When we stop resisting life's rhythm and start moving in time with it.

After pain comes the choice: cling to what hurt you or step into what heals you. Peace is that step. It is the place where we accept what was, stand steady in what is, and trust what's coming.

In this section, we lay down the weight we were never meant to carry. We stop chasing certainty and start choosing alignment. We learn that peace isn't something we wait for—it's something we claim.

This is where we breathe.

BLESSINGS DON'T ALWAYS COME DRESSED IN LIGHT.
SOMETIMES THEY ARRIVE IN THE DARK—
JUST TO TEACH YOU HOW TO SHINE.

MIDWEST SKIES

I wake up with my coffee. A day of fun ahead with my besties. But what they don't know is that I'm up to my neck in stress, holding in the pain I won't express. Because I have these walls—walls—walls that keep me up at night. Walking around the halls—halls—halls of my own head. But the walls aren't protecting me. They're wrecking me. Keeping me from what's ahead.

Because I won't say what needs to be said.

That I'm struggling. That I'm a mess. That I'm scared. That all I do is second-guess. Everything. Fearing I've royally fucked up. Worrying I've wasted too much time, money, and energy giving away my power... trying to fix what I think is broken—totally missing the point that nothing is a wreck.

Because this disco ball? She shines because of her broken pieces. She reflects the light not in spite of the fractures—but because of them. And yet, I forget. I always forget.

So when my besties ask if I'm OK—knowing I'm not because they feel the tension climbing up my neck, the energy that says I'm not fine—I try to hold the wall. Be strong. Stand tall. But I can't. And it bursts. I burst. I start sobbing so hard I can't breathe. Letting it all out. Crying so long, so loud, I can't remember the last time I let it all go like that.

These two women, sisters in spirit, hold the space. No judgment. Just presence. They let me fall apart, because they know that's what I need to do to come back together. And I say what I've been hiding: I'm afraid of the fall. I'm afraid of wasting it all. I'm confused by this call to burn it all down, to pick up a new crown. To grab a new pen and rewrite my story again—one where I make amends with the monsters in my head.

And as they gently talk me off that ledge, the clouds part. The ache softens. And for the first time in weeks, I feel something that's been missing: hope. Because there's something magical about a good cry with best friends who are your roots—the kind that steals your breath and returns your truth. The kind that cracks you open and calls you home.

That day, I stepped out into the warm Midwestern sky, eyes puffy, but heart light. Grateful to be alive. Grateful to be seen. Grateful to have these women by my side. Because sometimes the most broken moments are the ones that bring you back to yourself.

As my ego starts to die,
I am coming more alive—
truly feeling into my whole being,
dreaming even bigger
about what I am seeing,
and what might be possible for me.
As I set myself free,
stepping into who
I was born to be—
a real Queen Bee.
Suddenly,
surrendering,
and bowing down
to the possibility
of pollinating
something new.

THINGS TO REMEMBER NOT TO FORGET

1. Keep the main thing the main thing.
Your fortune lives in your focus, and what you focus on expands. Stay locked in on what truly matters, trust yourself, and let the noise fade away.

2. The people you hire aren't your friends.
Maybe someday they can be, but beware blurring the lines.

3. Clear is kind.
Say or do the hard thing, because if you think uncomfortable conversations are tough, the consequences of avoiding them are even tougher.

4. Tension is a deviation away from who you are.
Fear, stress, anxiety, jealousy, anger, doubt, boredom, pessimism—these emotions are signs that you're not living, being, or working in alignment with your authentic self. Pay attention when you feel tension, and recalibrate.

5. My way of living doesn't have to be yours.
We're all on different paths, and that's okay. Your dream doesn't have to look like anyone else's.

6. Don't be afraid to pivot.
Most people stay the same, phone it in, do/look/be the same thing decade after decade. Corporate Barbie robots. Take a risk.

7. Don't sell yourself. Be yourself.
Authenticity is magnetic. You don't need to convince anyone of your worth—just show up as you are, and the right people will find you.

8. You will always take you with you.
In other words, wherever you go, there you are. If you don't address the root of your struggles, no change of scenery will ever fix it.

9. Your life will mirror your emotional trends.
Clutter on the outside? Clutter on the inside. A best friend who treats you like trash? You're likely trashing yourself. You will always attract who and what you feel about yourself.

10. Beware the Money Grabbers.
There will always be someone ready to take your money, promising to fix what's broken or solve a perceived problem. While it's important to invest in your team and your growth, it's equally important to guard your power. Don't outsource the tasks that built you—those are the ones that shape your perspective and point of view. Instead, invest in areas that free you to focus on what truly matters. Remember: no one gets rich writing endless checks. Choose wisely, and keep your power where it belongs—with you.

When I go,
you better bury me in a hot pink suit.
Wait—
better yet, burn me in one,
because I'm going down
in fashionable flames, baby.
I want my wrinkles to prove I lived.
I want my tattoos to tell epic stories.
I want my scars to show how far I've come.
I want my laugh lines to outnumber my regrets.
I want to roll up to the pearly gates—
a little bit late,
buzzed,
and overflowing with
L O V E.
See,
this isn't a story about death.
It's a bop about life—
Because death isn't what ends us—
it's what reminds us to begin.

I AM INTELLIGENT
I AM HEAVEN-SENT
I AM RELEVANT
I AM MAGNIFICENT
I AM RESILIENT
I AM EVIDENCE
I AM CONFIDENT
I AM COURAGEOUS
I AM GROUNDED
I AM LUMINOUS
I AM MAGNETIC
I AM _____

Once upon a time,
the dark night
lasted a little longer
than she'd like.
But instead of resisting
this time,
she began accepting—
knowing,
expecting,
growing,
into a star
that lived high in the dark sky,
wondering why
she didn't see it the first time—
that she is the dark night,
because it always
turns into light.

FINDING YOUR "THING"

Anyone else want an answer to this question: "How do I figure out what my thing is?" I get it. We all want the North Star—that one thing that makes us feel alive, aligned, and unstoppable. But here's the truth: you don't find your thing by sitting still and trying to manifest it.

And while we're at it, can we talk about that word—manifest? It gets an eye roll, a woo-woo reputation, and rightfully so—because it's misunderstood. So let's understand the assignment: manifestation is not about sitting around like a Zen monk in full namaste energy waiting for things to fall into your lap like, "OMG, I'm hashtag blessed."

Real manifestation? It's giving your intentions attention.

You don't just think your dreams into being—you holler at them. You get clear on what you want, and then you take action. You make one brave, messy, meaningful move forward every day in the direction of your dreams. That courage becomes compound interest on your goals. So no—you don't "find" your thing by overthinking or waiting for a sign. You find it by doing. By moving. By being an active participant in your life and paying attention to what lights you up—and being brave enough to follow it, especially when no one else understands it yet.

Your "thing" doesn't have to be a business or a brand or some perfectly packaged life purpose. Sometimes your thing is your energy. The way you walk into a room. The way you make people feel. The way you model what's possible simply by being fully yourself. I don't know about you, but some of the biggest inspirations in my life are people who changed me just by existing—bright, bold, fully expressed. That's a thing. A big thing. A necessary thing.

And here's the other truth: your thing will change. Mine has. In my 20s, my thing was having fun with friends and building a career. In my 30s, it was climbing corporate ladders and mastering improv. In my 40s, it's been all about entrepreneurship and self-discovery. And now? My thing is self-expression. But I didn't figure that out by waiting. I figured it out by doing. By evolving. By paying attention.

So if you're still unsure of your "thing"? Don't panic. Follow your fascination. Notice what you talk about for hours without getting bored. What feels energizing—not exhausting. What you'd do for free. What feels like you—even if no one else gets it yet. Where you have natural enthusiasm.

Your thing isn't something you find. It's something you create.

even the fanciest
most prestigious museum
would be nothing but a void
without the people in it
because art only comes to life
when it meets the mind
of a person—
to give it perspective,
a point of view—
offering something new
filling in the void
with something true

SHE CAN'T COME WITH

The hardest part of growth isn't the becoming. It's the letting go.

Letting go of the version of success that no longer fits. Letting go of the approval you've been addicted to. Letting go of the comfort of predictability. Letting go of the old version of you—the one who can't come with.

And for me? That last one was the hardest. Because I love her. I'm so proud of her. And if I have to let her go, what does that even mean? Will I ever see her again? Will she know how far we've come? Will I ever get the chance to show her that we did it—that we became everything she always dreamed we'd be?

Because I'm gonna miss her. She sacrificed so much. She worked so hard. She's a beautiful, gentle soul, and I just want to hug her. Hold her. Keep her safe. Take her with me. Because I don't know if I can do this without her. She's always been by my side. And what—I'm just supposed to leave her behind? That doesn't feel right.

So yeah, the letting go is hard. And maybe that's why it's taken me so long. Because I didn't want to say goodbye.

But here's the truth: she's not gone. She'll never be gone. She lives in my soul now.

This journey began with 8-year-old Judi, and she still has a seat at the table. Every past version of me—the scared ones, the scrappy ones, the fierce ones, the fiery ones—they're all still here. They're my board of directors. My ride-or-dies. My soul sisters. My intuitive angels. My saving grace.

So as I pull myself out of the dark and step into the light, I don't walk away from them. I keep them safely to my left, as I turn to the right and step into the bright light.

I am the eye of the storm.
I am the stillness in the midst of motion.
I am the calm in the center of chaos.
I am the steady in uncertainty.
I am the line that will hold.
I am the anchor when it all unfolds.
I am the root when the winds take flight.
I am the dawn of a new day.
I am the sun on the other side of rain.

things are always working out for me
things are always working out for me
things are always working out for me
things are always working out for me
THINGS ARE ALWAYS WORKING OUT FOR ME
things are always working out for me
things are always working out for me
things are always working for me
things are always working out for me
things are always working out for
things are always working out for me
THINGS ARE ALWAYS working out for
things are always working out for me
things are always working out for me:
things are always working out for me
things are always working out for me
things are always working out for me
things are always working out for me
things are always working out for me
things are always working out for me
(always) me

THE MESSY MIDDLE

The messy middle is that brutal, beautiful space between who you were and who you're becoming. It's where the magic is. It's also where most people quit.

It's like, you're not the old you anymore. But you're not quite the new you either. You're in that liminal stretch of identity where nothing makes sense, your certainty's been yanked, your confidence is cracked, and every instinct tells you to throw in the towel and give up. But for the love of all things holy—don't. This is where it gets good. Not easy, but good. The middle is where the clarity comes. The tools sharpen. The real you forms. It's uncomfortable because you're growing. And growth? It's a demolition before it's a design.

And in the times when nothing's working, when it feels like you're getting nowhere—that's when you're developing the skin thick enough to handle it when it does work.

If I could go back and give myself one piece of advice during all of my messy middles, it wouldn't be to push harder or figure it out faster. It would be this: chill out. Relax. Go have fun. And while you're at it—take good notes. Document this process. Don't let yourself forget everything you're learning right now. Because what I've come to know for certain, is this: the universe will only give you more of what you're projecting. So your number one job? Feel good. As good as you can, as fast as you can. Why? Because when you feel like shit, you get more shit. When you feel stressed, you attract more stress. The good stuff you want can't find you until you're tuned to the same channel it's on. That's how energy works. That's how alignment works.

And trust and believe—what's meant for you will not miss you. Let that notion relax you. Trust where you are. Know that if doors are closing, they're meant to close—because something else is trying to open. God is just trying to get your attention.

The middle isn't the problem. Impatience is. Lack of trust is. The belief that you should already be "there" is.

No journey exists without pit stops, detours, or flat tires. Sometimes the GPS glitches. Sometimes the snacks run out. But you don't ditch the car. You pull over, stretch your legs, fill the tank, and keep going. The middle isn't a sign you're off track. It's proof you're on it. So take notes. Stay in the car.

Let the transformation work on you.

It comes in waves,
this silent battle I fight,
day after day,
night after night.
Why do I feel this way?
Cause it wasn't always …
this way ….
The crazy thing is,
I remember life before it.
I remember the freedom of just being,
not obsessing
over my fear of not breathing.
Elevators, planes,
hikes, stages,
long drives,
traffic, high heat—
man, I never skipped a beat.
Now I can't even take a walk in the street
without a checklist of extremes,
just to feel safe,
just to be,
just to do what used to come so easily.
Look, I can definitely see—
I'm a chess piece on the board of my own misery.
This childhood trauma I'm not looking at,
and the only reason I'm not looking
is that I'm afraid of what might look back.
Afraid to rehash the past,
not wanting that negative energy to clash,
with the peace I now have,
but the irony is,
it already has.
Because what you don't deal with won't heal.
Whether you like it or not,
life will sit you down and look you in the eye
until you finally see
what's holding you back from living free.
So I guess there's no looking back,
and the only way to address this
is to undress it,
so I take my power back
and clap back at this
panic attack.

THE HUMMINGBIRD

Your job in life is to be a hummingbird.

Have you ever watched a hummingbird? They flit from flower to flower, tree to tree, sipping nectar from each one—getting a little something different everywhere they go. They don't overthink it. They don't analyze every blossom before they land. They just move with curiosity and instinct, collecting sweetness and leaving behind what doesn't serve them.

Fun fact: hummingbirds can visit up to 1,000 flowers in a single day. They're tiny, fierce, and efficient—moving fast and staying fueled. They're built for exploration and powered by curiosity.

And that's how I believe we should approach life—especially if you're in your 20s, trying to figure out who you are and what lights you up. Be a hummingbird. Because how are you supposed to know what you like and don't like unless you go out there and actually try things? How will you know what you want to do, where you want to live, what kind of people you vibe with, or what foods you crave—unless you go out there and give it all a shot?

You can't read your way into certainty.
You can't think your way into knowing.
You've got to go live it.

I always say—how do I know what it's like to work with someone until I work with them? Same goes for life. How will I know if I like writing if I don't write? How will I know if I like entrepreneurship if I don't take a stab at it? How will I know if I like making music if I don't make music? How will I know if I love poetry if I don't start writing it?

Real talk: no one knows shit about shit.

You can read all the books, take all the courses, and follow all the advice, but nobody is you. You have to find your own nectar. You have to try different things and see what sticks. Practice. Patience. Time. Hard work. Consistency. That's the only algorithm that matters. You can't predict which flower's gonna hit—so taste them all. Like a hummingbird.

Keep moving. Keep sipping the sweetness.
Don't overthink it.
Follow the pull of your curiosity—and see where it takes you.

I move before I know.
I trust before I see.
I reach before I'm ready.
Just keep climbing.
Just keep climbing.
Just keep climbing.
Hang on tightly,
but tread lightly—
because it's likely
you'll find yourself precisely
right where you need to be,
despite blindly,
ascending highly,
divinely aligning,
finally finding,
what's always been,
quietly shining.

SUBTRACT TO ADD

In a world obsessed with more, more, more, we're conditioned to believe that success comes from doing all the things, all the time, all at once. We set big goals. Write long to-do lists. Slap together vision boards and hit the ground running. But let's be honest—no matter how organized we are, we run out of time.

While I pride myself on being goal-focused and strategic, I've realized something powerful: time bends when we practice subtraction. Instead of constantly adding goals, commitments, and expectations, what if we focused just as much on what we could subtract?

- How good would it feel to take things off your plate?
- What would shift if you reduced your workload?
- Imagine how it would feel to have fewer obligations cluttering your calendar.

I still have big, audacious goals. That's nothing new. But I'm shifting how I approach them. For every plan I add, I'm subtracting something else. Because focus is the real fortune.

I even do this with my closet. If I buy a new pair of shoes, a blazer, or jeans—something else has to go. Something in, something out. It keeps things intentional, clutter-free, and ensures I actually love what I own.

So as you sit down to map out what's next, don't just think about what you want to gain—think about what you need to let go of to make space for it.

Make a list.
Check it twice.
Then subtract to simplify.

Because success isn't about how much you can juggle—it's about having the clarity, energy, and bandwidth to move the right things forward.

If you give everything attention, you steal from yourself.

Your energy is finite.
Protect it.
Set boundaries.
Subtract to expand.

And watch how much more meaningful life becomes.

One thing I didn't realize I'd love
about moving to the desert
is that I'd never again hate
the clouds or a rainy day.
Even if I'm in Italy
or Greece,
or visiting a pyramid in the Middle East—
it could rain like cats,
it could rain like dogs,
it could rain all day,
it could rain all night.
But try as the rain may try
to put out my light,
it never will—
because now I have new sight.
And when we see things differently,
we feel things differently.
And when we feel things differently,
we do things differently.
So blame it on the rain—
the rarest gift in a desert sky,
the proof that water is required to grow high,
the nudge we need to take it slow,
the reminder of what it looks like to let it go.
So, yah, blame it on the rain,
because perspective
changes everything.

WILDFLOWER

One of my favorite rap lyrics of all time is by Lil Wayne: "Throw dirt on me, grow a wildflower."

Whew.

That line has lived in my bones for years. Maybe because that's exactly how I've felt for most of my life—like an underdog who never quite fit in, always told she was too much, constantly having to bloom through the dirt.

But here's the magic: wildflowers need the dirt. They don't just survive in it—they thrive in it.

They grow fast, they grow strong, and they grow everywhere. Some wildflowers can even bloom within 30 days of planting, bursting into color in the most unexpected places—sidewalk cracks, desert highways, rocky hillsides. You can pull them, prune them, stomp on them—and they still find a way to grow back, bolder than ever.

That's the energy I want you to channel. Not the manicured perfection of roses or the predictability of tulips. But the wild, defiant beauty of a flower that grows wherever the hell it wants.

Because your life doesn't need to be pretty or perfect to be powerful. The dirt you've lived through? That's your root system. The pain? That's your growth plan.

You don't want to be a wallflower.
You want to be a wildflower.

Pull a card
and
take a beat, Queen—
your dreams deserve
to be seen.
Light a candle,
catch a vibe,
and trust the timing
of your life.

They'll watch you. They'll copy you.
Poach from your table
and pretend they cooked the meal.
They'll drop your name—for gain.
Smile in your face,
then throw you under the train.
They'll mimic your magic
like they found it first,
sip on your style
to quench their thirst.
They are vultures.
Coyotes.
Always starving—
because imitation doesn't nourish the soul.
They'll shape-shift into besties, supporters, stans…
everyone's best friend.
Buying their way to the top,
calling it authenticity—
but the real ones know: they're a scam.
And yeah, it stings
to watch this scene.
Because you?
You're original.
You build from truth.
You move with integrity.
So when people pickpocket your essence,
it's personal.
But still—don't shrink.
Don't dim. Don't stop.
Let them study. Let them watch.
Because while they echo—you evolve.
While they repurpose—you know your purpose.
Your light doesn't need permission.
It needs protection.
Stay sacred. Stay sharp. Stay original. Stay real.

INTENTIONS + ATTENTION = MANIFESTATION

God continues to show me,
Spirit keeps serving up,
and I keep swerving into,

LESSONS

ON

LESSONS

My faith—often questioned,
but one thing stays refreshing:
my commitment to expressing,
never second-guessing
the way I'm progressing,
the talent I'm finessing,
the dreams I'm no longer suppressing.
Finally getting—
instead of preventing—
life's blessings.

LET THE PAINT DRY

I was watching a MasterClass with the iconic Futura—my all-time favorite graffiti artist—and somewhere between the spray can techniques and the stories of his come-up, he dropped a piece of wisdom that stopped me cold. He was demonstrating how to create lines and bleeds with paint when he turned to the camera and said: "Don't forget—let the paint dry."

He said it simply, but it hit like scripture.

Because what he meant wasn't just about technique. It was about patience. About giving the process space. About not rushing to the next thing just because the world tells us faster is better.

Futura went on to say that when he steps back and gives the work time to settle, he often comes back with a new perspective. A fresh idea. A new move he wouldn't have seen had he kept pushing through. And it got me thinking—how often do we sabotage our own brilliance because we don't give our souls time to breathe?

We live in a world that doesn't let the paint dry. We panic. We pivot. We don't want to fall behind or look like we're standing still. But some of our best work—the truest, boldest, most soul-aligned stuff—needs time to become.

I learned this the hard way.

When I first launched Holler at Your Dreams to the world, it fell flat. Instead of letting the idea breathe, I panicked. I took advice from the wrong voices—people who didn't get it, people who didn't get me. One even asked with a smirk, "So how's that working out for you?" Not out of care. Out of critique.

And I let it get in my head. I didn't let the paint dry. I repainted the canvas with someone else's brush—and it cost me. Time, money, energy, and worst of all, trust in my own vision.

So if you're reading this right now? Please. Let the paint dry.

Let your vision breathe.
Step back.
Take a beat.

The masterpiece can't be rushed—and neither can your soul.

So there I am, en route to a keynote,
feeling like a kid on Christmas—this job is so dope.
Fresh off the plane, totally ready to go,
travel isn't easy, but I've found ways to thrive on the road.
The plane lands, I pull up to the gate.
A car is arranged. A hotel awaits.

As we drive, I think—how I always forget my room number.
Seriously, I don't care what anyone says, they all look like each other.
First order of business? Unpack.
Line things up neat like bread in a stack.
Most rooms feel stale and smell like a stranger,
so candles and crystals help me change that—which is major.

I finally settle in, ready for the night to begin,
when I notice it feels lonely—dare I say, almost ghostly?
It needs some color, a spark, some light,
something to soften the weight of the night.
I reach for my leopard-print emergency bag.
Whoever said traveling smart can't be chic anyway?

I carry office supplies. I'm always prepared.
A bit much? Maybe— but today, I'm glad I nerd out that way.
A Sharpie. A stack of pink Post-its.
Quickly penning power anthems like I'm Guns & Roses:
You were born to shine.
You are a star.
You get standing ovations.
You've come so far.
Each note, a lifeline—
quieting my mind like a glass of fine wine.

Morning breaks—a fresh new day,
a chance to make waves, a new chance to slay.
Outfit's on lock. Bags are repacked.
Rested, rehearsed, I'm ready to rock.
Time to check out. But before I leave,
I thank my room for its role in my day,
for keeping me safe while I stayed—when I spot them:
the Pink Post-it Power Ballads.
Forgotten? Maybe. But divine? Absolutely.
Because they're not coming with me.
They're staying behind—
a gift for the next soul who needs a sign.

I never know who sees my dope love notes,
but I like to imagine they spark some hope.
Because the world shines brighter when your light is on—
and this?
My little way to…
pass it on.

GRAFFITTI POP

In high school, my dad built a bedroom for me in our basement. It was nothing fancy, but to 16-year-old me, it was everything. Yo—I even had a Swatch phone, a waterbed, and a TV in my room. It was a total 90s dream.

The drywall on the outside of the room never got finished. But instead of bugging my dad to close it up, I let it ride. And slowly, me and my high school friends turned that wall into a graffiti masterpiece. Quotes. Signatures. Inside jokes. Song lyrics. Doodles. Teenage confessions. Four years of scribbled memories turned that unfinished wall into a living, breathing time capsule. It was our story—raw, loud, unfiltered.

And when I look back now, I realize: that was my first love letter to graffiti. And to myself. Graffiti is so much more than spray paint on a wall. It's art with a pulse. It's poetry in motion. It's a creative revolution.

Here are 10 reasons graffiti is an oracle:

1. It breaks rules—but within a powerful code of honor that keeps expression safe and sacred.
2. It turns pain into power. So many artists start with heartbreak and transform it into something beautiful.
3. It's loud. Not always in volume, but in presence. You can't ignore it.
4. No two pieces are the same. Because no two people are the same.
5. It doesn't wait for permission. Graffiti doesn't knock—it declares.
6. It's for the people. Created outside traditional systems, it lives on streets, trains, and bridges—and speaks to everyone.
7. It's soul-led. Most graffiti artists didn't go to art school. They just picked up a can and started expressing.
8. It lives in color. Bold. Vibrant. Unapologetic. Graffiti doesn't ask to be muted.
9. It makes forgotten spaces unforgettable. Graffiti transforms decay into beauty.
10. It redefines art. Like my hero Futura once said, his abstract style confused people at first—because they couldn't define it. But over time? He created his own lane.

I love graffiti. It's messy and moving. Wild and wise. It reminds us that our expression is valid—even if it doesn't follow a blueprint.

Especially if it doesn't.
Because boxes are for packaging, not people.

She's

Sweet and savage
Scared and brave
Confident and nervous
Ready and apprehensive
Grounded and guarded
Strong and soft
Excited and anxious
Bold and vulnerable
Expressed and exposed
Creative and unsure
Discomfort and joy
Fierce and gentle
Visible and afraid
Hopeful and hesitant
Resilient and tired
Healing and still hurting
Becoming and unlearning

She's

both // and

HOW TO FIND YOUR DREAM

So many people wait for their dream to show up like a neon sign. But in reality? Dreams usually arrive as whispers. Nudges. A quiet tug on the soul. Here's how to begin listening:

1. Listen to your whispers.
Your dream might not be shouting at you—it might be whispering. Pay attention to what keeps popping into your mind when things are quiet. What would you do if you had no fear, no judgment, and no limits?

2. Beware comparing.
Your dream doesn't have to look like anyone else's. It doesn't need to be big or flashy to matter. The only thing it needs to be is yours. Whether it's creating a happy home, running a marathon, or starting a garden, it's valid.

3. Look at what lights you up.
Think about the things that energize you or make you lose track of time. What makes you feel alive? Your dream might already be hiding in the things you love—but haven't prioritized.

4. Explore what's missing.
Sometimes your dream is tied to what you crave. What feels absent from your life? More connection? Creativity? Peace? Fulfillment? Your dream could be as simple as taking steps to invite more of that into your world.

5. Get clear on what you don't want.
Sometimes, clarity comes through contrast. What's draining you? What's holding you back? What's making you feel small? Clearing the clutter often helps your dream emerge.

6. Give yourself a green light.
Your dream is worthy—no matter how big or small it seems. If being a present and joyful parent is your dream, own it. If moving to your dream destination is your dream, embrace it. Stop waiting for permission. Your dream is enough because you are enough.

Let this be your reminder: Your dream matters. It doesn't have to be clear, perfect, or grand—it just has to be yours. Dreams live in your soul. Goals help you bring them to life. And if you don't know what your dream is yet, that's okay. The first step is giving yourself the time and space to listen, explore, and uncover it. So, what's whispering to you right now?

I only look forward—
because I can't go back.
To words that cut,
to vibes that lack
alignment
with who I am now.
So
I take a bow—
to all the dirt that made me a flower,
to all the storms that shaped my power,
to every lesson my past self met,
reminding me that
I AM
always the best bet.

Repeat after me ...

I guard my vibe with my life,
because I know the quality of my mind
directly fuels my ability to grind.
I understand there will be highs
and lows—
that's just the way life goes, so,
I do the work,
even when the vibes are high—
especially when the vibes are high.
That's how I stay in flow
when things get low—
especially when things get low.

I keep my aura clean.
Pristine.
As fly as a photograph
in Vogue magazine.
With boundaries,
a deep trust in my intuition,
and a mad respect for red flags.

I surrender.
I slow my roll.
I know who to let go—
and who to promote
into roles in my life
that align with the healed version of me.
While I drop the dead weight of those
who don't.

I'm here to be who I was born to be—
Fully.
Freely.
Confidently.
Without apology.
An icon.
The one and only.
Me.

LET IT BE YOU

There are a lot of things that annoy me about social media—but then there are humans like Tabitha Brown who make the scroll worth it. She is like a warm blanket for your soul. A walking, talking hug. One of the best storytellers on the internet.

Especially when I'm riding one of my low waves or having a dark night of the soul—she's the page I navigate to like an Oracle deck, letting whatever message I land on be the one I'm meant to receive.

Case in point: I was having one of those particularly low days when I stumbled across a video that stopped me in my tracks. I was in a season of my business where things weren't moving fast enough. And if I'm being honest, I was scared. Scared to be in the full expression of myself. Scared of how the world might react—or worse, not react at all.

In the video, Tabitha was being interviewed on a podcast. The host asked her, "How did you learn to embrace yourself to the point where people and brands basically build things for you?"

She answered: "I got tired of pretending. I got tired of trying to fit in. I got tired of pretending to be somebody that was not. I said, 'Okay God, I'm gonna show up and be who you made me to be.' And I think the obedience to trust Him and show up as who He created—you get rewarded for that."

That's it right there. Obedience to your soul. Trust in your design. Courage to show up even when no one else gets it yet.

That's the thread that's helped me break cycles—out of toxic environments, low-vibe thinking, financial struggle, and fear. It's the same thread that runs through Self-Expressionism. Because when you stop editing yourself to be more palatable, when you stop dimming your light to be more digestible, you create alignment. And alignment creates peace. And peace unlocks momentum.

So if you needed the reminder today—this is it: You don't need to fix who you are. You need to trust who you are. And then? Let it be you.

Because when you show up as the version of yourself that God dreamed into existence, you will be rewarded.

Manifestations
are the result of you being you—
fully attuned,
following the clues,
listening deeply,
moving with soul,
letting that inner pull
guide you home.
Always arriving
right on time,
your life becoming
the ultimate rhyme—
as you finally understand:
the real assignment
was never hustle.
It was always
alignment.

OPINIONS AREN'T FACTS

SWEET SURRENDER

I used to think surrender was bullshit. Like, "Cool for you, mystic on a mountain, but I've got bills to pay."

As a control freak in recovery, the idea of surrender always felt... vague. Soft. Mystical in a way I didn't trust. I couldn't wrap my head around how I was supposed to "let go" and still run a business, lead a team, build wealth, hit deadlines, stay accountable, and survive the world. Surrender felt weak. Passive. Like giving up.

But now I know better.

And if I can learn to surrender—you can too.

Because surrender isn't doing nothing. Surrender is choosing faith over fear. It's trusting the process more than you trust the pressure. It's letting go of the white-knuckle grip on the way it has to happen so that something bigger—something better—can unfold.

See, control is just a mask for worry. When we grip too tightly, we block the very thing we're trying to create. Surrender is opening your palm. It's stillness with strength. It's movement without mayhem. It's a deep inner knowing that says: I'm doing my part—and trusting Life to meet me halfway.

Here's what that looks like in real life:
- I speak faith, not fear.
- I catch the better thought, even when doubt is louder.
- I trust the unfolding, even in the pause.
- I get to feeling good—fast. Because when I feel good, I attract more good.

If you want to feel what surrender actually feels like, try this: Close your eyes. Extend your arm. Make a fist and squeeze it tight. Hold it. Clench harder. Feel the pressure build. The discomfort rise. The tingling. The resistance.

Now—release it.

Feel that? That is surrender. You didn't disappear. You didn't quit. You're still here, still whole—you just let go of the pain.

And now your hand is open.

Which means something beautiful can finally land in it.

Aging ambitiously is her secret weapon—
life dishing out lessons,
wrapped in blessings,
making growth her only obsession.
She officially declares—
she will no longer waste her time.
She puts herself first in line,
remembers that she is a dime,
and not doing this is the only crime.
She arrests her fears,
her doubt, her tears,
the thought that she's wasted years—
when she is, in fact,
right on time.
So perfectly imperfect.
So wildly divine.
Aging like fine wine.

FEEDBACK

Not every opinion is wisdom. And not every piece of feedback deserves your energy. In a world obsessed with advice, feedback, and being "coachable," it might sound wild to say this, but here it is: don't listen. Not to everyone. Not all the time. Not when your peace is on the line.

This is sacred strategy.

Because the more you crowdsource your life, the more you disconnect from your own clarity. You second-guess what you already knew. You start making moves that please others but betray your truth. That's how originality dies.

Some of the best advice I ever received? Was the advice I didn't take. The people telling me how to dress, what to write, what to tone down or change—and I didn't listen. And thank God. Because that choice not to listen was the best advice I ever got. It kept me aligned. It kept me whole.

And sometimes, not listening means protecting your process.

I'll never forget when I was sharing behind-the-scenes video on social media during a season of making music. A friend gently pulled me aside and said, "Hey Judi, what if you kept that offline? Like… don't let them see you coming. Just drop the album one day and be like: you're welcome." Yo. That hit me like a truth bomb wrapped in a hug.

In a world addicted to oversharing, there's something revolutionary about privacy. About letting your soul make something without needing an audience for every step. About holding the sacred for yourself before handing it to the world. Yes, seek support—but only when you're looking for affirmation, not direction. Don't ask people to give you your perspective. That part is yours. Others can enhance it. Shape it. Refine it. But the magic is already in you.

When you know better, you flow better.
When you know better, you flow better.
When you know better, you flow better.
When you know better, you flow better.
When you know better, you flow better.
When you know better, you flow better.
When you know better, you flow better.
When you know better, you flow better.
When you know better, you flow better.
When you know better, you flow better.
When you know better, you flow better.
When you know better, you flow better.
When you know better, you flow better.
When you know better, you flow better.
When you know better, you flow better.
When you know better, you flow better.
When you know better, you flow better.
When you know better, you flow better.
When you know better, you flow better.
When you know better, you flow better.
When you know better, you flow better.
When you know better, you flow better.
When you know better, you flow better.
When you know better, you flow better.
When you know better, you flow better.
When you know better, you flow better.
When you know better, you flow better.
When you know better, you flow better.
When you know better, you flow better.
When you know better, you flow better.
When you know better, you flow better.
When you know better, you flow better.
When you know better, you flow better.

YOU REAP WHAT YOU SEED

Looking back, I can trace the storm of 2023 and 2024 all the way back to who I was in 2021 and 2022. And whew—21/22 me? She was chaotic. I was ungrounded, reactive, arrogant, lost. I let my ego get too loud. I was chasing shiny things. I wasn't practicing what I preached. I was off.

And guess what? I got exactly what I planted.

The garden of your life doesn't lie. Your external world is a reflection of your internal one. If you plant bitterness, you grow resentment. If you plant ego, you grow burnout. If you plant chaos, you grow confusion.

But the same is true in reverse. Plant peace? You get clarity. Plant truth? You get alignment. Plant love? You get it back tenfold.

This isn't about being perfect. It's about being aware. Your thoughts are seeds. Your energy is soil. Your attention is water.

So... what are you growing?

Because what you plant today becomes your life tomorrow.

I'll never forget the time
someone delivered our turkey
on Thanksgiving Eve—
so we had food to eat.
I was probably eight,
maybe nine or ten,
and I knew right then
the extent of what it meant.
I remember looking at my dad
right in the eye,
and for the first time in my life,
saw shame instead of pride—
but also deep relief,
knowing his family would eat
with the help we just received
from people who were strangers to me.
Now every Thanksgiving,
no matter how old I get,
I remember that moment—
I'll never forget.
I've made it tradition
to help others the same way
those strangers did for us that day,
back when I was eight.
It's moments like these
that shape who we came to be.
Because flash forward to today—
almost 40 years later—
I can still see this neighbor,
this stranger,
so clear.
As I peer out the window,
watching with wide eyes,
like a deer in headlights—
full of wonder and fear,
as our meal appears.
Totally reliving
the real definition of
Thanksgiving.

THE KEY TO LONGEVITY

The key to longevity in business, original thinking, expressionism, art, ideation—and honestly, the pursuit of any creative act—is openness.

Openness of mind. Openness of heart. Openness to possibility. It's the opposite of victimhood. It's choosing to see life as happening for you, not to you. It's that classic improv mindset: Yes, and…

It's being faced with a mountain you didn't expect, looking up at the summit and resisting the urge to say, "Yo—I don't climb mountains. I'm not a mountain climber. This isn't my jam." Instead, it's rolling up your sleeves and going, "Welp… I guess we climb mountains now. Let's go."

And when you do climb it—step by messy, unsure, courageous step—what happens? You reach the top. You see farther. You gain new perspective. You open up an entirely new landscape of possibility for yourself—one you couldn't even fathom from the ground.

That's the brilliance of experience. The gift of failure. The wisdom in trial. Because every time you climb a new mountain—whether it's personal, professional, emotional, or existential—you leave the old you behind and take in the view with new eyes.

So stay open.
Risk the climb.
Because the view?
It's always worth it.

She makes a graceful nod to the night,
as her hair blows in the wind,
standing tall on her feet,
looking up toward the light,
at the stars in the sky—
finally knowing,
that she was, is, and always will be,
alright.

SOULWAVE

There's this cool little trick I stumbled upon one day—totally by accident—that made me go, whoa. I was in my Photos app on my iPhone, just scrolling, when I pinched the screen in with my fingers. Suddenly, my entire year in photos collapsed into one view. A tiny, vibrant mosaic of moments. It almost looked like a frequency soundwave—a visual hum of my life in living color. A snapshot of my soul. My movement. My presence over the course of an entire year. It looked like it had a pulse.

There was hot pink. Energy. Lots of blue sky. Color on color on color. Living proof that I've been alive—creating, connecting, expressing.

So now, I want you to try it.

Here's how:
- Go to your Photos app.
- Tap "Albums."
- Select "All Photos."
- Then pinch the screen in to zoom out.

Boom. There it is—your year at large.
Your life at scale. Your soulwave.

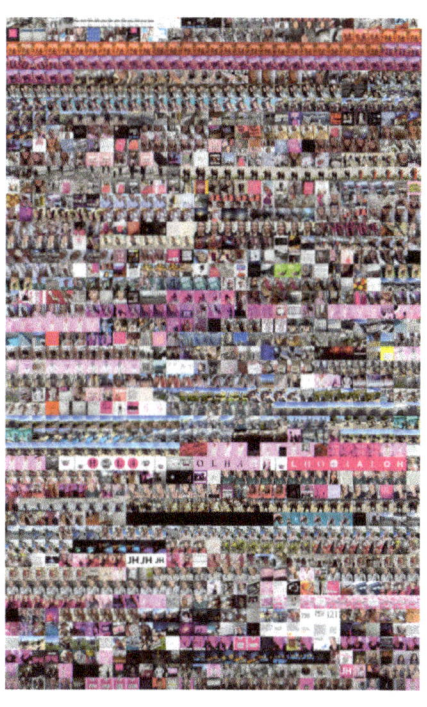

Now ask yourself: What story does this image tell? Is it bright? Monochrome? Blurry? Bursting with color? Is there a dominant hue? What energy does it radiate? What season does it reflect? Could the colors in your camera roll reflect the aura you've been putting out into the world? Is there joy in the frame? Movement? Memory? Or are you longing for a new rhythm? A deeper shade? A wilder hue?

This isn't about aesthetics—it's about awareness. A creative way to audit the color, the cadence, the fullness of your life. And if you don't like what you see?

Good news: you can always paint with a new color.
You just have to fill the screen with it.

I didn't think I'd miss the seasons so much—
the rainstorms of spring,
the sweet smell of freshly cut grass in summer,
the scent of apple pie beneath a crisp autumn sky,
the slow snow days of winter,
forcing you to stay inside.
While I love living out West—
a new playground to self-express,
the desert healing me in ways I'd never guess—
I still have a longing for the Midwest.
My roots.
My soul.
My bones.
Where I spent 45 years.
So it's no wonder I'm here,
but part of me is still there—
a soft longing for what was familiar,
for the nostalgia,
a sliver
of what used to be.
Or—
maybe I'm homesick.
Or—
maybe I just miss
parts of the old me
that built this me.
Knowing growth is the game,
and it was time for a change—
the desert calling my name.
Feeling glad I came,
but still missing the rain.

BUILDING BELIEF

You just need one believer—but that believer has to start out being you.

Here's the thing—research shows that most people won't do anything uncertain or uncomfortable with confidence unless they genuinely believe they can. This is a concept called self-efficacy, coined by psychologist Albert Bandura. Self-efficacy is belief in one's own ability to succeed, and without it, you're basically stuck at the starting line.

So, how do you build belief when you're feeling low on confidence? There are three ways—and you don't need all three. Just one will do. Let's break it down:

- Vicarious Experiences: This is the art of borrowing belief. It's watching someone else do something hard, scary, or seemingly impossible and realizing, "If they can do it, so can I." It's the classic proof-of-possibility move. If he can run a marathon, you can run a marathon. If she can write a book, you can write a book. Seeing others succeed makes it more believable for you.

- Verbal Persuasion: This one's all about someone else pumping you up—motivating you to take action. Maybe it's your spouse, your mentor, your bestie, or even a speaker who lights a fire under you. It's someone you respect telling you, "You've got this." And because they believe in you, you start to believe in you. Sometimes you just need that hype squad to give you the push.

- Mastery Experiences: My personal favorite. If you've read my first book Fear Is My Homeboy or seen one of my keynotes, you know I'm obsessed with this idea. It's all about doing something hard yourself and living to tell the tale. This is where fear experiments come in—intentionally doing things that scare you to build your courage muscle. Each time you do something difficult and make it through, you build proof that you can do hard things. You become the evidence. This isn't just a cute motivational quote; it's actual facts: She believed she could, so she did.

If you're struggling with belief right now or need to rebuild it, start here. Pick one method and give it a go. Because all brave moves begin with belief.

DON'T BE MORE OBSESSED WITH THE ALGORITHM THAN THE RHYTHM OF YOUR OWN LIFE.

I'M NOT FOR SHOW.
I'M FOR SOUL.

LOVE BOMB

I'm always looking for ways to feel good—fast.

Because when we feel good, we attract more good. That's the game. And to win it, we've got to get out of rumination, overthinking, self-doubt, and negativity as quickly as we can. The goal? Shift into optimism, hope, belief, and enthusiasm—the frequency we want to be in.

So whenever I catch myself spiraling, I play a game.

I call it The Love Bomb Game—and it works every. single. time.

Picture this: I'm driving. I'm in a bad mood. I'm pissed off about something that happened. Instead of stewing in frustration, I start love bombing everything I see.

- I love my car.
- I love the sun.
- I love this song.
- I love the palm trees.
- I love my nail color.
- I love the desert mountains.
- I love Chipotle.

LOVE BOMB YA FACE OFF.

It works.
It shifts your focus.
It gets you feeling good—fast.
And that's the whole goal.

Good or bad,
God always has a plan.
Regardless of what happened in the past,
It's time to free yourself in the present—
with the present
of presence.
You are on the path.
I can promise you that.
Deep breath.
Trust where you're at.
Holler back.

PRACTICE, NOT PERFECTION

I've been building a new keynote for two years. It's been uncomfortable, frustrating, and honestly, humbling as hell. My old talk was fire—it took me seven years to build and three years to perfect on stage. Standing ovations, laughs exactly where I wanted them, feeling like an actual rockstar every single time. But as I evolved, I knew I needed to create something new—something that matched who I was becoming.

But I forgot something major: I had to be a beginner again. I had to give myself permission to suck for a little bit. To try, fail, adjust, and practice. I found myself beating myself up for not being as smooth, confident, or seamless as I was used to being. I was trying something new, but I was stuck in the mindset that it needed to be perfect right now.

Then it hit me: Practice.

Doctors practice medicine. Psychologists practice therapy. Lawyers practice law. Artists practice their craft. Musicians practice scales. Athletes practice drills. Yogis practice poses. Writers practice writing. Pilots practice simulation flights. Even chefs practice recipes before they land on the menu.

So why was I holding myself to an impossible standard of instant perfection? Why was I obsessed with being flawless rather than being a practitioner? That mindset shift was like flipping a switch, and suddenly, it all made sense. I was building something new. Of course it wouldn't be perfect. I needed to practice, not perform.

Every time I step on stage, I'm refining, experimenting, tweaking, and learning. And you are too, in whatever it is you're building. Your art. Your business. Your craft. Your life.

So, here's the takeaway: stop being obsessed with perfection and start being committed to practice. It takes the pressure off and lets you show up curious, brave, and open to growth. Practice your craft, your art, your life. Let the pressure mold you into the gem you're becoming—but never let perfectionism rob you of the joy of becoming. Be a practitioner, not a perfectionist. That's how you'll get where you're meant to go.

Worrying worships the problem.

Trust worships the process.

You get what you spit.

    S O

Your words are wands.

    S O

What spells are you casting?

    A n d

Does it correspond to …

    The future that you want,
    The presence that you need,
    The past that must leave—

So you can finally breathe.
And really be,
Fully free.

FAKING IT

I think "fake it till you make it" is the trashiest of all trash advice on the planet. It's dangerous. It's reckless. It's lazy. It's inauthentic.

Because when you fake it, all you're doing is attracting things that aren't really for you—the real you, that is. This is how we end up miserable, exhausted, overwhelmed, and stuck. It's like wearing someone else's shoes and wondering why you aren't walking right.

Now, I get it. This phrase usually comes from good intentions. People are trying to tell you to be brave, to put yourself out there, to do what you gotta do to make it happen. And I love that sentiment. But let's be real—this language is confusing, and it often sets us up to perform instead of progress. It leads us to pretend instead of become.

The real flex these days? Make it until you make it.

Go all in on what only you can do. Double down on what makes you, you. Be the only version of yourself that exists—sooner rather than later. That way, you start attracting the right people, the right clients, the right opportunities, and the right vibes sooner than later. Man, I wish someone would've taught me this in grade school. Instead, I was dissecting frogs and solving equations I would never use—when I could've been getting schooled on the real talk of life: how to be unapologetically myself.

This is why I could never be you and you could never be me—and that's a good thing. This is why copying others will never work. This is why "faking it" is dangerous. This is why the healers, the crystals, the coaches, and the courses only get you so far—because if something doesn't belong to you, it will not stay with you.

In a world that feels anything but authentic, the real flex is to be authentic.

And you do that by making it until you make it.

They don't see her comin'—
but she's runnin'
straight for the mainframe,
ready to pull the plug
and turn off all the noise.
So loud.
So loud.
When did everything get so loud?
She can barely hear her soul anymore.
Who does she wanna become?
Where does she wanna go?
What is it she needs to know?
So loud.
So loud.
She's got to turn down all this noise.
So she can scratch that itch,
and be that bitch.
A glitch in the matrix
who reroutes the system.
Logged out to tune in.
Tapped in to turn on.
Amplified to turn up—
her own power source.

MOST PEOPLE

Most people are other people.

Oof. That Oscar Wilde quote hits, doesn't it?

And it hits because it's true. Most people are other people. Their opinions? Borrowed. Their preferences? Hand-me-downs. Their passions? Just echoes of someone else's voice.

I watched a video the other day—this woman was talking about how her favorite color had always been purple. Then she paused and asked herself: Is it really? Turns out, her mom loved purple. Their house was full of it. And because she loved her mom, she adopted purple as her own. But then she realized... she also loved green. And pink. Maybe purple wasn't hers at all. Maybe it was just inherited.

That got me thinking. How often do we mistake influence for authenticity? How much of what we love, believe, and claim as "ours" is just a reflection of someone else's preferences, expectations, or validation?

Maybe you've been told you're a great cook. You don't actually like cooking, but because you're good at it, you convince yourself you must love it. Do you? Or did someone else hand you that identity?

This isn't just about colors or hobbies—it's about everything. The music you play. The dreams you chase. The values you hold. The way you define success.

And guess what? It's supposed to evolve. What mattered to you at 20 might feel irrelevant at 40. What you once thought was your life's purpose might have been a stepping stone—not the destination.

So, sit with yourself. Ask the hard questions. Strip away the noise until you find you. Because before you can be anything—a CEO, an artist, a leader, a badass—you have to be yourself first.

Love—
it always comes back to love.
So like a dove,
I float above
doubt, insecurity, feeling unworthy.
No longer an imposter,
or assuming imposter syndrome's a monster.
I call it what it is—
a sign I'm ready to begin.
To win.
So I put down my violin,
no longer a victim to past sins,
or worried about future chagrins.
Instead,
I feel ready to fly. To try. To aim high.
Because— love.
It always comes back to love.

SOUL KNOWS

There will be moments in your life when logic is loud, but your gut is louder—and learning to trust that difference is everything. On paper, something might look right. But inside? You feel it. A subtle tightness. A weird energy. A flicker of knowing. That's not fear. That's information. And that's where your true compass lives.

Your gut is your guardian angel. Your intuition is your primary brain. Your inner voice is your real power source. Logic has a place—it helps you think through the options. But intuition? That's where your truth lives. It's not random. It's sacred. It's soul curriculum.

So how do you trust your gut when your mind is spiraling?

You pause. You listen. You stop crowdsourcing your clarity and start honoring your own. And most importantly? You give yourself space. You let the waves of emotion settle. You stop rushing the answer. You play a little hard to get with your own decision-making. You let your inner knowing rise to the surface instead of forcing an answer to show up.

Sometimes it's a full-body hell yes. Sometimes it's a clear no. But often, you're in the messy middle—that liminal space where clarity takes time. That's not indecision. That's sacred timing.

When I'm in that space, I grab a piece of paper. I draw a line down the middle and make two columns: pros and cons. I let it all spill out. My brain likes that structure. But the truth? My gut already knows which column is louder. It always has.

These days, I let my intuition lead. Even if the outcome isn't perfect, it's still right.

Because when you trust your gut, you're not just making a decision—you're obeying your soul. And that kind of alignment? It always pays off. Sooner or later, it becomes wisdom.

Slow and low
that is the tempo—
even though
it feels like the opposite
of how she was conditioned to flow:
Always on the go.
Never saying no.
Listening to ego more than soul.
But she finally let all that go.
Now she's trusting her bones,
armed with a vision board
and a mission.
This time, she's not stuck in submission.
Or wasting time wishing—
she's getting back to living,
life as God planned it.
The only her on the planet.
Solid like granite.
No longer frantic—
now she moves like magic.

Don't let the noise of the world drown out the voice of your *soul*

LEAVING WHERE YOU ARE

Over the past few years, I've felt myself shifting. Growing. Becoming. Like there was this poetic, electric, wildly dope part of me—neon-lit and beat-driven—that had been lying dormant for far too long. I craved her. I missed her. I needed her. I am her.

The things I've created in the world have always made me proud. No regrets. But I could feel something new rising. A new body of work. A new keynote. A new conversation. A new crown with my name on it.

Still, I was terrified to walk away from what was working—specifically, my old keynote and the stories I'd been telling on stage for eight years. They built me. And abandoning them? That felt dangerous. Like a betrayal.

So I brought in a mentor I collaborate with on my keynotes. She always gets me unstuck and adds a beautiful, swaggy substance to my work. We jump on a call, and I begin setting the stage for this expansion—sharing all the fears I'm having about how scared I am. What if this doesn't work? What if no one gets it?

She lets me rant, then takes a beat and says:
"Judi, you've brought me in because you want to go somewhere new. Is that correct?"

"Yes," I whispered.

"Then, my girl... you're going to have to leave where you are."

Oof.

She was right. If we want to go somewhere new, we must leave where we are. That doesn't mean abandoning what built us—but we do have to reinvent it. Reimagine it. Realign it with who we are now. Because if you want to leave, you've got to lead. And that begins with you because you are the one who's going.

So go, guided by the rhythm only you can hear.

I just want to be me.
Can't you see?
If only you were brave enough to set me free—
maybe, just maybe,
you'd get what you want after all:
Someone not afraid to make the call.
Someone in it for the long haul.
Someone who goes all in when the moment calls,
wears the goal like a jersey—
number bold, name tall.
No need to compete.
No room for drama's sharp teeth.

I just want to feel safe.
Can't you see?
If only you'd let me make mistakes—
maybe, just maybe,
you wouldn't have to explain:
Why everyone wants to escape.
Why no one's engaged.
Why we've lost our aim,
and misplaced our faith—
in systems that chase
output over input,
compliance over creativity,
urgency over humanity,
rules over realness,
metrics over meaning.

I just want to have fun.
Can't you see?
If only you'd lighten up—
maybe, just maybe,
you'd tighten up
morale, retention, results.
Make work feel like a container,
instead of a cage, with,
Support over surveillance.
Soul over silence.
Play over perfection.
People over performance.

Dear Corporate America—
Don't be afraid.
See me. Trust me. Grow me. Know me.
Because when I feel safe enough to self-express,
I will bring my best.
And when I bring my best—
work starts working again.

I KNEW IT WAS GRACE
BECAUSE YOU CATCH ME WHEN I CAN'T.

LOOKS GOOD VS FEELS GOOD

So much of life is spent chasing what looks good—what impresses, what's expected, what gets applause. But at what cost?

If you're feeling anxious, stuck, lost, or uncertain, here's a simple but transformational journaling exercise that might just shift everything for you:

1. Draw two columns on a blank page.
2. Title the left column: Looks Good
3. Title the right column: Feels Good
4. Now, get real. Write down all the things you do because they look good—things that are externally validated but don't necessarily bring you joy or peace.
5. Then, in the right column, write down what actually feels good to you. The things that light you up, ground you, and align with your truth.

Here's an example to get you started:

Looks Good	Feels Good
Posting daily to stay "relevant"	Taking a break so your mind can breathe
Responding instantly to every message	Letting your inbox breathe with support systems in place
Saying yes out of guilt, fear, or habit	Saying no with love, and yes to your capacity
Working nonstop to prove you're worthy	Resting to remember that you already are
Hustling for likes, claps, or validation	Creating from your soul, even if no one claps yet
Building fancy funnels that drain you	Designing a business that sustains and reflects you
Looking busy in your calendar	Making space to actually think, create, and live
Following trends to stay in the game	Following your rhythm to change the game
Saying "I've got this" when you're drowning	Asking for help and letting yourself be human
Chasing what "they" say success is	Defining what success feels like to you

This isn't about throwing everything in the "Looks Good" column away—sometimes what looks good also feels good. But if you're constantly running on empty, it might be time to shift focus. Because the only person who truly knows what feels good? You. Take the time. Ask yourself. And align accordingly.

i love the way
you self-express —
a beautiful ritual
for cleaning up the mess.
so never second-guess
your redefinition of success.
go within,
reassess,
and let what heaven sent
rise up to manifest.

SLOW MONDAYS

I love a slow Monday.

It's become a sacred ritual I protect at all costs. And while no week is perfect—sometimes I'm flying, traveling, or jumping on a client call to close business—95% of the time, Mondays are mandatory reset days. I don't take calls. I don't schedule meetings. I don't record content or hop on Zoom. Mondays are mine.

Instead, I ease into the week with intention. I review my calendar, do light admin, and carve out space to think—to actually work on my business, not just in it. I soak in the luxury of moving at my own pace, often still in pajamas until I leave for my afternoon workout. This is one of my favorite parts of entrepreneurship: the freedom to design a schedule that optimizes my energy instead of depleting it.

To make it even sweeter, I bookend the week with a Freestyle Friday. It's a buffer before the weekend—space to catch up, wrap up, or do whatever the week calls for. Sometimes I write. Sometimes I run errands or play hooky. Sometimes I do absolutely nothing. It's less about checking boxes and more about checking in—with myself, my needs, and the rhythm of my work.

These two rituals—Slow Mondays and Freestyle Fridays—have changed my work life. They give me the margin I need to show up strong the rest of the week. They create a soft start and gentle close, which has made me more creative, more productive, and way less burnt out.

And isn't that the whole point of building a business?

To build something you don't need a vacation from.
To build a life that feels like yours.

Steal this idea.

You don't need to earn rest. You need to protect it.

Like the wind,
it blew in—
intuition.
So she leaned in
and listened,
as it whispered
her mission.

MOST PEOPLE WON'T

Most people won't change or reinvent or grow. Most people keep doing things the same way they've always done them—because that's the way they've always done them. Why? Because growth is hard as hell. Reinvention demands you suck for a while. It requires you to be a beginner again. It forces you to lay down your ego and pick up the paint.

Case in point: as a keynote speaker, I built a talk that crushed. It took four years to refine—four years of live reps, edits, failures, and feedback before it became the buttery, soul-hitting experience it is today. That talk lit up rooms, got standing ovations, and booked more gigs than I could count. Once it clicked, it felt like slipping into a custom suit. I knew every beat. It made me feel like a rockstar. But then I outgrew it.

I felt myself changing. Evolving. And I knew my talk had to evolve with me. My old material didn't fit anymore—t felt like performing a role I had quietly outgrown. So in the spring of 2022, I started experimenting. I played with new ideas, fresh stories, poetry.

And let me tell you—it was awkward. It was humbling. It was uncomfortable as hell. I kept wondering, "Is this missing the mark? Should I go back to what works?" But then I remembered: this is the lab. This is the creative process. And it's supposed to feel like this when you're stretching into something greater.

Most people won't tolerate that kind of discomfort. Most people won't trade certainty for creative fire. Most people won't let themselves be new again. But if you want to grow—really grow—you have to be willing to suck. You have to be brave enough to stay in the room with your own becoming.

So if you're in the lab, stay there. Don't quit because it's not perfect. Don't tap out because it's not yet smooth. Keep building. Keep believing.

Because most people won't—but you will.

Wuddup God
It's me, ya girl, Holler.
Thank you for this brand-new day,
For the breath in my lungs,
And the light in my way.
I ask for your grace—
To forgive my missteps of yesterday,
The moments I fell short,
The times I lost my way.
Help me be stronger and do better today.
I pray you place the right people,
The right places,
And the right opportunities in my path.
Give me the wisdom
To know when to step back—
When what's in front of me
Isn't here to help me slay,
But to distract, detour, or lead me astray.
For your guidance, your grace,
And your love every day,
In your name, I pray.

Amen.
HOLLAlujah.

10 WAYS TO FIX YA ENERGY

Feeling off? Energy low? You don't have to stay stuck. Energy shifts fast—when you know how to move it.

Here's how to fix your frequency and get back to feeling good, ASAP:

1. Get Green: Plants aren't just pretty—they clear the air, boost your mood, and bring life into your space. Science backs it: greenery reduces stress and increases happiness.

2. Charge Up Your Crystals: Better yet, let the full moon do the work. Crystals store and amplify energy, so keep them close, cleanse them often, and let them remind you of your own power.

3. Bask in the Sun: Natural light = nature's antidepressant. Open your windows. Step outside. Take a walk. Set a timer for 10 minutes and let the sun hit your face.

4. Phone a Friend: Energy is contagious—so call the one who gives you life. Good vibes transfer through WiFi.

5. Light a Candle: Because fire transforms. Candles shift the mood. Set an intention, light it up, and remember: even the smallest spark can brighten the dark.

6. Declutter Your Space: Messy space, messy mind. Studies show clutter spikes stress levels and lowers focus. Clear the chaos, clear your head.

7. Ground Yourself: If you can't get your feet in the grass, do this: rub your hands together fast for 15 seconds, pull them slightly apart, close your eyes, and feel the energy pulsing between them. That's your actual frequency. Buddhist monks used this technique to find peace in prison. If they could do it in a cell, you can do it in the concrete jungle.

8. Buy Yourself the Roses: Roses have the highest vibrational frequency of any flower. Put them where they'll inspire you daily. (Fresh roses measure at 320 MHz—yes, really.)

9. Dance It Out: Turn up your favorite playlist and shake your ass. Let the beat remind you to take one.

10. Write Down 10 Things You're Grateful For: Because gratitude is so gangster and it's the fastest way to shift from what's missing to what's already there.

WORDS CREATE ENTIRE WORLDS.

CHOOSE WISELY.

Can we please glamorize growth?
And the faith it takes to swear an oath—
to purge oneself of childhood wounds,
the kind that whisper you missed the moon,
as you gaze at stars
that feel so far,
wondering if they only shine
to remind us that we can too, in time.

Can we please glamorize growth?
And the courage it takes to swear an oath—
to let go of the need for control,
the force that quietly steals your soul.
Replacing it with a trust that lies within,
a compass drawn by divine intuition.
Your God-given mission already known,
inner wisdom guiding you home.

Can we please glamorize growth?
And the guts it takes to swear an oath—
to purge oneself of doubt,
to reclaim the power you've given out.
To trust that this dirt, this heavy shower,
will shape you into a radiant flower.
And just like rainbows after the storm,
the sun will rise, its warmth reborn.

Fear is a shadow
lurking near—
but courage softly
whispers in my ear:
Hey baby, you got this.
Stay in the zone.
All this discomfort means you're almost home.

NO MISTAKES ONLY GIFTS

In our house, this phrase gets tossed around almost daily. Because there always is one—a gift, buried beneath the muck. Even in the shittiest of shit, if you're willing to dig deep enough, there's usually a golden nugget that will make you better.

"No mistakes, only gifts" is something I first learned on the improv stage. In improv, mistakes aren't setbacks—they're springboards. A flub often gets the biggest laugh because it's human, real, and completely unplanned. Just like life.

But let's pause. Because I know what some of you are thinking: "Easy for you to say. I'm a surgeon. I'm an airline pilot. I work in compliance. I can't afford mistakes." And you're right. In your world, the cost is higher. You train harder. You prepare relentlessly. And you carry the kind of responsibility most people can't imagine.

But even in those high-stakes spaces, the principle still applies. The operating room isn't where the mistake should happen. But somewhere along the way—on a cadaver, in a simulation, during training—there were missed marks. Fumbled tools. Incorrect steps. That's how mastery is built.

Mistakes, when properly placed, are the reason people get good at what they do. Without them, there's no innovation. No sharpened instinct. No wisdom.

I've made plenty myself:
Said yes when I meant no.
Signed bad contracts.
Ignored my gut.
Stayed too long. Bit my tongue. Outsourced my power.
Trusted the wrong people. Judged too quickly.
Told white lies to keep the peace.

And that's just the highlight reel.

But every time, I walked away with a gift: a sharper edge, a clearer truth, a stronger sense of self. These days, I move slower. I sleep on decisions. I trust my gut more than the noise. And I only sit at tables that match my frequency.

So how about you? What "mistakes" are you still holding onto that may actually be preparing you for mastery? Write them down. Name the gift.

The real flex isn't perfection. It's awareness.

NO ~~MISTAKES~~ MISTAKES.

ONLY GIFTS.

If the devil can't stop me,
he'll distract me with—
doubt,
insecurity,
jealousy,
perfectionism,
self-sabotage,
and resentment—
that steals my contentment
for this version of myself
that I haven't met yet,
because I'm too caught up
in the casualties
of lost confidence.
So, instead of taking forward steps,
I second-guess
this knowingness that's in my chest.
But this time,
I close my eyes
and take a breath,
coming back home to center—
remembering that
I'm heaven sent.

INVISIBLE STAIRCASE

Once you start building invisible staircases for yourself, you'll get obsessed.

Trust me.

The invisible staircase is a mindset—a way of moving through the world rooted in faith, not fear. It's the idea that with every brave step you take, the next one reveals itself. Not before. Not all at once. One. Step. At. A. Time.

And it's not just a metaphor. It's how real progress happens.

Here's the truth: none of us have a script. Life is improv. Everyone—everywhere, every day—is climbing an invisible staircase. The difference? Some people like it. They trust the process. They get curious. They climb even when they can't see the top. Others stay stuck at the bottom, paralyzed by what they can't control, refusing to move until they know what's next.

One response sets you free. The other keeps you in a cage.

The happiest, most successful people I know climb anyway. They take swings. They make mistakes. They look cringe. They practice. They put themselves out there. They don't wait for permission or perfection. They just keep moving. Because they know: movement creates momentum.

Momentum reveals the next step. That's the game.

So if you're in the space between where you are and where you want to be, let this reframe set you free: stop waiting for certainty. Start moving with curiosity. Be willing to be surprised. You don't need to know how it ends to begin.

Just start climbing.

may she never become so obsessed with the

algorithm

that she loses the

rhythm

of her soul.

FORTUNE COOKIE

It wasn't even my fortune cookie—but it still hit me straight in the soul.

I was watching an entrepreneur share his story of growth on stage when he mentioned a fortune he once pulled from a cookie. It read: "When you tell the truth, you don't have to remember anything."

And whew. That one landed.

Because one of the biggest ways I've messed myself up—in life and business—is by not being as open and honest as I should've been. I've bitten my tongue. Blurred lines. Stayed silent when I should've spoken up. Not to lie—but to avoid discomfort. I feared the conversation more than the frustration I was quietly choking on.

See, I grew up in a house where things exploded. Lamps were shattered. Words were weapons. Conversations? Nah. We had confrontations. So I learned to avoid truth if it meant keeping the peace.

But here's what I know now: when you avoid the truth, you don't avoid the consequence. You just delay it—and make it worse. What could've been a five-minute conversation becomes a five-month spiral. What could've been clean becomes chaos.

I'm learning to choose courage over comfort. Truth over tension. Because open and honest isn't just a vibe—it's a lifeline.

So if you're sitting on something—say it. Clear the air. Have the conversation. You don't need to carry the weight of pretending everything's fine.

Tell the truth. It's lighter on the other side.

You are never too late.
 You are not too old.
  There are 365 days
   A N D
    365 ways
     To find your way back home.

THERE YOU ARE

You can hire the coach. Join the mastermind. Redesign your office. Burn the sage. Read the book. Move across the country. Reinvent your wardrobe. Reorganize your life. But if you're not connected to yourself—if you're not in alignment—none of it will stick. It'll feel good for a minute, sure. Like a high. A fresh start. A clean slate. But eventually, the same patterns creep back in. The stress. The self-doubt. The urgency. The overthinking. Because the truth is: wherever you go, there you are.

I know because I've lived it.

I thought moving from the Midwest to the desert would change everything. New life, new me, right? But I was still me—just with palm trees instead of oak trees. I brought all my old fears with me. All my blocks. All my limiting beliefs. Change of scenery, same inner script. And that's the danger—confusing reinvention with avoidance.

I've learned that growth doesn't come from running. It comes from remembering. From returning. From re-rooting in who you really are.

So if you're tired of chasing clarity, maybe it's time to sit still. To look in the mirror. To come back home to yourself. Not some upgraded version. Not some perfectly healed, fully optimized self. Just you. As you are. Because when you're rooted in that? Everything you build from there has a chance to last.

THE PRESENCE

"DEFINING MYSELF,
IS LIKE CONFINING MYSELF,
SO I UNDEFINED MYSELF,
TO FIND MYSELF."
IN-Q

(BE IT)

Presence is not about performing—it's about being. It's where we stop measuring ourselves by titles, roles, or expectations and start embodying who we truly are

After pain, after peace, comes this: the moment. The only one we actually have. Presence asks us to show up fully, not as a version of ourselves edited for approval, but as the raw, undefinable, unrepeatable force we are meant to be.

In this section, we shed the need to prove and step into the power of simply being. We learn to trust our instincts, honor our energy, and own the space we take up.

This is where we arrive.

YOUR TALENT IS SICK,
SO DON'T GET IT TWISTED.
YOU GOTTA STAY LIFTED,
AND NEVER FORGET—
YOU ARE GIFTED.

YOUR MISSION IS TO BE SO REAL THAT FAKE

PEOPLE ARE UNCOMFORTABLE AND THE

REAL ONES ARE INSPIRED.

FINDING YOUR VOICE

I once read that it takes an artist an average of 7 to 10 years to find their voice. But I don't think that's entirely true. I think it takes an artist 7 to 10 years to trust their voice. To stop shape-shifting. To stop trying to sound like everyone else. To stop asking for permission to be bold. And to start believing that the sound of your soul is more than enough.

Finding your voice isn't about stumbling into a fully formed identity—it's about building the muscle of self-trust. It's about training the courage to show up—raw, loud, weird, wild—and letting the work get good by letting it get real. You experiment. You improvise. You fall on your face. You keep going. And somewhere in that messy middle, you stop asking, "Do I belong?" and start declaring, "This is who I am."

It took me a lifetime to claim the last name I was born with—Holler. It had always been there, waiting. But I wasn't ready. Not until I had done enough living, learning, and letting go. Not until I built the intuition and initiative it would take to stand fully inside of it. And when I finally said yes, it was a full-body YES. Not because someone told me to—but because I knew it in my bones.

That's the magic of finding your voice.
It's not about volume—it's about vibration.

When it's really yours, it echoes. So if you're still experimenting... good. Keep going. Get weird. Be brave. Make messes. Your voice will meet you where your courage lives. And when it finally shows up, don't forget: the point isn't just to find it. It's to trust it.

And then—let it holler.

This isn't midlife—
it's main character energy.
Unapologetic.
Unbothered.
Unleashed.
She's not aging—
she's ascending,
writing her name
in uncensored fonts
on every blank page
that ever dared call her "too much."
She's in her prime,
a certified dime,
right on time,
holding on tight
as she welcomes the light
of
49

THREE PILLARS OF SUCCESS

Success isn't just about talent—it's about alignment. True momentum comes when your skills, personality, and beliefs are working together. When all three are in sync, you become unstoppable. But when one is off? You feel stuck. Frustrated. Like something's missing and you can't quite name it. So how do you create real alignment? Start here—your three pillars:

1. Your Skills
What are you actually great at? Not the stuff you wish you were good at—the stuff that flows from you naturally. Maybe it's writing, problem-solving, storytelling, managing chaos, or building trust. Maybe it's memory, intuition, or charisma.
Ask yourself:
- What do people consistently ask me for help with?
- What feels easy to me but hard for others?
- If I had to teach one thing tomorrow, what would it be?

2. Your Personality Traits
Your natural vibe shapes how you work and lead. Some people thrive in structure, others in spontaneity. Some light up in front of a crowd; others bring the magic behind the scenes. Knowing how you actually operate—not how you think you should—is a game-changer.
Ask yourself:
- What do people consistently compliment me on?
- What's the energy I bring into a room without trying?
- What kind of environments drain me—and what kind fuel me?

3. Your Beliefs
Your beliefs are the filter for every decision you make. If you believe you're not ready, you won't show up. If you believe failure is fatal, you won't take risks. But if you believe in growth, in learning, and in your ability to figure it out—you'll become a force.
Ask yourself:
- What/Who am I for? Not for?
- Do I trust myself to recover when things go wrong?
- Are my beliefs pulling me forward—or holding me back?

Here's the truth: Alignment is power. When your skills, traits, and beliefs click into place, you stop chasing—and start attracting. You move differently. Decide faster. Create momentum without burning out. So ask yourself today: Where am I out of alignment? And what small shift would bring me closer to my true self? Because when you get this right? Life starts to flow.

She's a flow-getter,
a trendsetter,
a spicy chili pepper,
a big bettor—
on herself.
Stacking chips,
never losing grip
of who she is,
who she was,
and who she's always been.
Destined to see
her name in lights,
her future bright,
her courage lurking in the night,
as she prepares to take flight.
Into the unknown—
because she's not alone.
She's got an army of angels,
a symphony of sisters,
a tribe of trailblazers,
too bold for danger.
As she rearranges her life—
clearing out the clutter,
setting boundaries like no other.
SETTING BOUNDARIES LIKE NO OTHER.
Did I stutter?
No, I didn't.
My priorities are on purpose,
Because my purpose is worth it.
So I keep my calendar pristine—
because my dreams reign supreme.

DIRECTIONS

When I was in the thick of it—birthing something new, something wild, something so mine it made me nervous—I did what so many of us do: I asked for advice. I asked people I love. I asked people who love me back. I asked people whose lives I admire—but wouldn't want. People who aren't even in the arena I'm trying to play in. People who, though well-meaning, are not experts in the thing I'm building.

And you know what their "advice" did?

It made me second-guess what I already knew.
It made me quieter when I needed to be bolder.
It made me tweak things that were already working.
It made me shrink the dream to fit someone else's idea of "reasonable."

Here's the truth: if you ask for too many opinions, you'll get talked out of your own voice. And that is the most dangerous thing you can lose. Because people can only advise you from their level of experience, from their fears, and from their frameworks—not yours.

So beware of taking directions from someone who's never been there. And if you're asking advice from someone who wouldn't even want the kind of life you're building, you're asking the wrong person.

Ask for support.
Ask for love.
Ask for someone to hold your hand while you leap.

But don't ask for directions from someone who's never walked your path.
You don't need permission.
You need perspective.
Yours.

When you finally unleash
What's been inside,
Screaming—"Please, let me out!"
Something wild happens.
Doubt dissolves,
And you remember what you're all about—
Knowing God doesn't make mistakes.
So you
take your cake—
and eat it, too,
Because this one precious life
is up to you.

I am because they think I can't

SHAPESHIFTING

We must know thyself. Because when we truly know ourselves, we can be ourselves. And when you can be yourself, you can lead yourself. But the inverse? That's where things fall apart.

When you don't know who you are, you end up shapeshifting—squeezing into boxes that were never built for you, saying yes to things that make you shrink, leading yourself into places that drain your magic and leave you wondering why you feel like a shell of who you once were.

Shapeshifting isn't strategy—it's survival. And it's not sustainable.

Yes, we all change and grow. What you wanted at 25 may not align with what you need at 45. That's why self-expression is a lifelong practice. You've gotta unplug from the matrix, sit with yourself, study your Human Design, experiment, explore, and be wildly honest about what's for you—and what's not.

Because the world doesn't need a watered-down version of you. The world needs your whole self. Your most creative, courageous, fully expressed self.

That's where your power lives.

I don't let anything,
or anyone,
define me.
I DEFINE ME.
I am defined because I am me.
   Divinely me.
      Designed to be who I came to be.
Destined to bravely holler at my dreams.

MOMENTUM

Feeling stuck doesn't mean something's wrong with you. It just means you've been sitting in the waiting room too long—overthinking, overplanning, and under-moving. And if you want to get out of that loop? Stop trying to fix everything. Just focus on one thing.

Fear hates when you do that, by the way. Fear loves when you're scattered, unfocused, and overwhelmed. It thrives on messy desks, cluttered calendars, and too-long to-do lists. Because when you're overwhelmed, you stay exactly where fear wants you—stuck. Safe. Scared. The same.

But when you get focused? When you get clear, even for five minutes? Fear panics. Because clarity leads to confidence, confidence leads to movement, and movement leads to change. And change? That's fear's worst nightmare.

So the antidote to stuckness is always motion. Even if your knees are shaking like Bambi. Even if you don't know what happens next. The simple act of movement—any movement—writes a new story. One door opens the next. That's how it works.

You don't have to run the marathon today. Just lace up your shoes. You don't have to write the whole book. Just open the doc. You won't pay off debt overnight. Just save the first dollar. You don't need the plan. Just take the next step.

When I'm stuck, I start a voice memo and talk to myself. I riff. I ramble. Sometimes I write to music and let the rhythm move me. Sometimes I lift weights. Sometimes I text a friend who gives off momentum like Wi-Fi. That's all it takes. Because momentum isn't just magic—it's generated.

So get in the way of something.
Start small.
Focus on next, not all.

She was born to transform—
to rise, to shift,
to shatter the norm.
To glow through the cracks,
to dance through the storm,
to reintroduce herself
in every new form.
At this age, unashamed,
as she turns a new page.
Her story? Hers—
to remix and rearrange.
A legacy too wild to cage,
too bold to tame.
She's her own sage,
stepping into her flame—
bravely,
boldly,
finally,
unchained.

BIRTHDAY

Every year on the morning of my birthday—before I scroll, sip, or step into celebration mode—I do one thing first: I write my future self a letter.
I find somewhere sacred (read: dreamy AF). A spa. A cozy hotel. A dope balcony. A spot that makes me feel like the main character. I open my laptop, hit compose in Gmail, and type the subject line: "Open on your [insert age here] birthday."

Then I write to the next version of me.

On my 45th birthday, I wrote to 46. On my 46th, I wrote to 47. This year? I wrote to 50. And whew—she is that girl.

In these letters, I hype her up. I tell her what we did this past year, how we felt, what we learned, what we let go of. I cheer for her like I'm front row at her concert. And once I'm done, I hit send—and snooze it to land on next year's birthday.

Only then do I open the letter I wrote myself last year. And let me tell you: it always hits. Sometimes I laugh. Sometimes I cry. Sometimes I cringe. Most of the time? I'm blown away.

This year, I read about a few things I was sure would happen in my 48th year. Spoiler alert: they didn't. A few big shiny doors I wanted to kick open? Slammed in my face. But here's the twist—I'm so glad they did. The things I thought I wanted would've taken me off track. What didn't happen protected me. And it reminded me that just because something doesn't come true today doesn't mean it won't tomorrow. Sometimes rejection is redirection wearing a power suit.

That's the magic of this ritual. It's not about perfectly predicting the future. It's about casting a bold, messy, beautiful vision. It's about honoring who you've been, loving who you are, and setting the vibe for who you're becoming.

Because every birthday is more than cake and candles. It's a reset. A sacred wink. A personal New Year's Day. So light your candle. Make the wish. Write the letter.

TRUST YOUR DOPENESS

HOW TO BE MORE CREATIVE

Creativity doesn't always strike like lightning—it can, but more often, it's something you practice, nurture, and build like a muscle. If you're feeling stuck or uninspired, here are seven ways to wake up your magic:

1. Take Yourself on Creativity Dates
(Shoutout to Julia Cameron via The Artist's Way.) Once a week, take yourself out—solo and on purpose. Try something new, go somewhere interesting, or simply give yourself space to think. Hit a museum, hike a new trail, find a new coffee shop. Every time I do this, I walk away with new ideas, stories, and a fresh perspective on how I want to show up in the world.

2. Unplug from the Matrix
The algorithm's got us in a chokehold. Get out. Daily, weekly, monthly—whatever your rhythm is, step away from the noise so you can hear yourself. Social media is not your muse. You are.

3. Write Down Your Ideas
Sounds basic, but most people don't do it. My Notes app is a digital vault of IP—quotes, bars, prompts, poems, verses. Your ideas are your property—capture them before they vanish.

4. Make Intuition Your Primary Brain
Your first idea is usually your best one. The second, third, and fourth are often your ego creeping in. Move with the initial spark. Your gut knows before your logic does.

5. Live an Interesting Life
Interesting ideas come from interesting lives. Read more books. Take more walks. Travel to new places. Talk to new people. Creativity thrives on exposure, not isolation.

6. Watch MasterClass
I'm obsessed with learning from legends—whether it's graffiti, poetry, music, or art history, I treat MasterClass like my personal creative lab, soaking up world-class wisdom one class at a time.

7. Have Audacity
This is the secret sauce. The audacity to hit publish. To post, share, speak, and show up. This is how you go from hiding to being heard. You don't need permission. You need nerve.

Creativity is a lifestyle. Stay curious.

DO IT BECAUSE THEY DOUBTED YOU.
DO IT BECAUSE GOD ROUTED YOU.
DO IT BECAUSE YOU ARE YOU.

ON THE GREEN

I think the greatest sporting event of all time here in the States—hands down—is The Masters.

Now before you roll your eyes or start falling asleep, stay with me. Yeah... your girl loves golf. I'm not any good at it (yet), but I hope that changes with age. That's one of the sneaky reasons I love it—if you're healthy, you can play for decades. I know women at our club in their 60s and 70s killing it on the course—looking fly as hell while doing it. And I literally can't wait to have my own golf cart.

I digress. Ok, back to the Masters ...

What I really love about The Masters? Phones aren't allowed.

Spectators can't bring cell phones or devices onto the grounds. That means no scrolling, no posting—just presence. People are watching. Listening. Breathing it in. It's like a giant phone-free sanctuary. A full day in nature, disconnected from the noise, soaking in the moment. I wish more moments in life were like that. Because presence? Is the real flex.

I recently took a 30-day break from social media —and it was magic. I needed to hear my soul, not my mind. That's hard to do when you're stuck in the scroll. I was writing this book, feeling annoyed with the platforms, and knew I needed to reset. Spoiler Alert: Social media doesn't help when you're anxious. It only amplifies what you haven't healed.

So I stepped away—from the algorithm, and back into my own rhythm.

Here's what happened while I was gone: I finished edits on this book. Delivered three keynotes. Studied Human Design. Organized my closets. Walked more. Called my friends more. Read more. And when I came back, I felt clear. More grounded. Refreshed.

Social media's not the enemy—but the algorithm isn't neutral. Meta spends billions learning how to keep us addicted. But what sustains us isn't in our phones. It's outside. So, go play.

SOUL > SCROLL.

She's giving main character energy,
seriously auditing
who gets accesss to her vibe.
Because she knows she is golden.
Beholden.
Super dope.
And worth knowing.
Her aura's locked in tight—
only the bold get to stand in her light.
As she moves doubt to the side,
confidently casting herself
as the leading lady
in her life.

REINVENTION RESUME

If there's one thing I've learned, it's this: betting on yourself is never a bad idea. Reinvention isn't a fluke—it's a decision. Over and over again. And everything I've tried, tested, and tinkered with on this journey? It's not failure. It's my reinvention résumé.

I've been the speech meet champ, the high school hostess with pom-poms, the comms major-turned-bartender who stumbled into corporate life and climbed the hospitality ladder. I moved to Chicago, joined an association, became its president, and moonlit as an improviser at Second City—eventually auditioning my way into the professional conservatory. That's when everything cracked open.

I started speaking on branding and improv, realized I could build a business, and launched HOLLA! Productions. I saved. I hustled. I said yes to everything. Then came the turning point: I was on my honeymoon, reading Big Magic, when Fear is My Homeboy was born. I left my corporate job, wrote the book, and hit the stage in head-to-toe hot pink. And it worked. Then, the world shut down.

In the aftermath, I pivoted—virtual events, new ideas, new lanes. I launched a planner. Experimented with life alcohol-free. Built a community. Branded an apparel line. Hired a five-figure branding agency. Started dreaming of global disco ball world domination. I was chasing all the shiny things—but somewhere along the way, I lost myself.

So, I moved to the desert. Got quiet. Hired a creative director. Launched a course. Dug deep. And what I found was the loudest, clearest truth of all: I was never off track. Every experiment, every pivot, every "what was I thinking?" moment brought me right back home to myself. I learned that the scattered energy I sometimes felt wasn't a flaw in my design, but instead my system's way of searching for what truly deserved my deep attention.

And if that sounds familiar—if you've been spinning, doubting, shifting—I hope this gives you hope. You don't need a perfect plan. You don't need everyone's approval. You just need the guts to keep reinventing. Because reinvention isn't a crisis. It's a calling.

And one day, all those messy, beautiful chapters will add up to something you never saw coming: a life that makes you proud.

I officially give you permission...
To change.
To grow.
To glow.
To flow.
To let 'em know.
To lose control.
To take it slow.
To drop your ego.
To soften like snow.
To miss the goal.
To say no.
To let it go.
To be whole.
To come back home.

She watches
as I put a layer
on my face—
to cover what's underneath.
AND
as I see her
seeing me,
I wonder—
what does this teach
a young girl
about her world,
AND
all she'll have to face,
as I cover mine
with makeup brushes
that now
feel like weights.

NOT FOR EVERYONE

Not everyone's going to get it. And that's the whole point.

If you're for everyone, are you really for anyone? Because trying to please everyone is a guaranteed way to dilute your magic, kill your momentum, and confuse the people who are actually meant to ride for you.

In a world full of noise, clarity is queen. You've got to have a perspective. A stance. A vibe. A filter. You've got to be willing to proudly exclude the people who aren't for you, so the ones who are can actually find you.

And please hear me—this isn't about politics or religion or stirring the pot (unless that's your lane). I'm talking about standing firm in your energy. Owning your voice. Declaring what you're here to do and how you roll so there's no confusion when someone walks through your metaphorical door.

Think about it like this: A restaurant sign that says No Wi-Fi. Talk to each other. You know the vibe instantly. A boutique that plays 90s hip hop and pours tequila shots on Saturdays—you know if it's for you or not. A business that says We don't do discounts—we do quality. Clear as day.

It's a big world. Let people know what they're walking into.

Because the real flex isn't trying to win the 99%. It's knowing who your 1% is—and having the guts to build for them.

So show up fully. Loudly. Clearly. Let the people who get it, get it. Let the rest scroll on by. Your job isn't to be understood by everyone. Your job is to be unmistakable to the right ones.

She fits like a glove,
and I instantly fall in love—
not just with how I look,
but with how I feel inside.
Confidence wraps around me,
beaming, bold, and bright.
I step aside,
let my outfit shine—
but what I don't yet realize:
the star waiting to rise
was never the clothes,
it was always mine.

EGGS WITH A BADASS

Before I had a book of my own, I had You Are a Badass by Jen Sincero. And when I was keynoting bringing improv volunteers on stage, I'd hand them her book as a thank-you—for the courage to put themselves out there. It wasn't just a prize. It was a proclamation: You are a badass! And I meant it. I've probably given away hundreds of copies of that book. I adore it. Still do. It's relatable, punchy, powerful—and when I sat down to write my first book, Fear Is My Homeboy, I knew that's how I wanted it to feel. Jen's book became my model for it's structure, tone, and bold truth-telling. Needless to say, I've been a mega fan for years.

So when I found out she was coming to Hudson, Ohio—the tiny town I was living in at the time—for a book signing in 2018, I registered without hesitation. The event was on a Friday, and I happened to be speaking in California earlier that week. I'd be flying home just in time. That afternoon, while waiting to board my flight home from Cali... I spotted her. Jen. Freaking. Sincero. At my gate! We were both headed to Ohio—me going home, her to the book event I'd be attending that exact night. (omg!) So, with all my courage I walk right up to her, introduce myself, and tell her how much her book changed my life. Total fangirl moment—but I didn't care. The universe had handed me a moment, and I wasn't about to fumble it. She was kind, gracious, cool as hell. No, we didn't sit next to each other on the plane (I wish!), but we landed, and that night, I got my book signed and floated home on cloud nine.

Fast forward to 2021. I get booked to keynote a major women's event—thousands in the audience. I'm chatting with the planner, going over the run of show, when I see it. Jen Sincero. Not just on the lineup. Speaking right before me. I lost my mind. The last time I saw her, I was still in corporate. Dreaming of being a full-time speaker. Writing my first book in my head. And now? We were sharing a stage. As peers. And I had a book of my own —one I could physically hand her as a thank-you for the inspiration she didn't even know she gave me.

We reached out to her team, hoping for a quick hello. She said yes. And not just to a backstage hello—she sat down and had breakfast with me!! So, in a hotel lobby in Utah, I had eggs with Jen Sincero. It was one of the most full-circle, soul-igniting moments of my professional life. But even more than that, it was a reminder of what happens when you bet on yourself. When you keep climbing those invisible staircases, even when you don't know where they lead And here's the kicker: while you are always your own ultimate muse, it's powerful to look ahead. To find people whose work lights a fire in you—not to copy, but to stay inspired.

I gave her book away for years, promoted her work without her ever knowing I existed. And I truly believe it was that no-strings-attached generosity that boomeranged this magical moment into my life. So stay real. Stay generous. The universe is always listening.

She's spicy.
Maybe that's why I've always liked her.
She's top shelf.
Maybe that's why I always feel like myself.
So as I sip this Cadillac,
in the shadows of Camelback,
I feel like I can finally paint
my canvas back from black.
Unpacking the facts
that helped me bounce back.
Turning set-backs
into soundtracks—
a throwback,
but really,
my comeback,
salted rim,
soul intact.

THE COST

You can have anything you want—but it will cost you who you are now.

When I was waiting tables in my 20s, I wanted to be a bartender. So I started thinking, moving, and carrying myself like one. I studied the bartenders, learned from them, networked with them, showed up as if the job was already mine.

Then I became a bartender.

As a bartender, I wanted a steady job—one with benefits, regular hours, and an office. So I shifted again. I started thinking like someone who worked in sales. I went to networking events. I talked to my bar regulars about their careers. I prioritized job searching and adjusted my schedule to create space for opportunity.

Then I landed my first hotel sales job.

In that role, I wanted to climb the ladder. So I showed up like a National Sales Manager—taking initiative, being easy to work with, speaking up in meetings, mentoring teammates, volunteering for projects, winning awards.

Then I got promoted to National Sales and moved to Chicago.

From there, I set my sights on becoming a professional speaker. So I stepped into the mindset of someone already doing it. I spoke at industry events. I networked with speakers. I read books, took improv classes, hired coaches, and saved money to fund the dream.

Then I became a full-time keynote speaker.

Once I started speaking, I wanted to write a book. So I began moving like an author—reading about writing, researching publishers, taking courses, asking for introductions, and saving for the project.

Then I became an author.

It's impossible to evolve with the same habits, mindsets, and energy that built your past. Every next level of your life requires a new version of you. To get there, you'll have to confront the parts of yourself that can't come. The comfort zones. The excuses. The limiting beliefs. This isn't just about career goals. It applies to everything—finding love, starting a business, healing your body, retiring early, living debt-free, or designing your dream life.

So ask yourself: Who do you have to become to get what you want? How does that version of you think? Speak? Move? What do they tolerate? What do they let go of? What risks do they take? What do they prioritize, protect, pursue?

Reinvention isn't about pretending to be someone else. It's about fully stepping into who you were always meant to be.

Life lately has been—
writers' rooms, poetry slams,
neon notebooks bursting with plans.
Dark basement bars that smell like nerves,
as voices rise
from all walks of life,
stepping up to the stage,
grabbing the mic,
seeking a spark to ignite—
a future that feels right.
This is all new,
because I am new.
But if I'm being honest with you—
it's what I've always wanted to do.
So, as I step into
a brand-new decade of dreams,
I feel reborn and ready—
to take the stage in new ways,
no longer afraid
of the fear in my face
trying to throw shade.
They say if you want something different,
you gotta do something different.
I've always known this to be true—
but lately,
it finally cuts through.
officially on a path of self-discovery.
No patience left for the cutlery
of words meant to silence
the softest of hearts.
I'm done hiding,
done dimming,
done shrinking in the dark—
ready to build a symphony
that plays a brand-new melody.
The main instrument?
Authenticity.
Unapologetically.

SHAMELESS

If we don't know who you are, what you do, what you stand for, or what you're selling... how can we help you? How can we hire you, buy from you, promote you, or recommend you?

You want to grow? You've gotta be seen.

Self-expression requires self-promotion. It's not optional—it's essential. But I get it—self-promo can feel cringey and ick, especially when it's dripping in "look at me" energy. You know the vibe: "Look how cool I am. Look how skinny I am. Look how busy and award-winning I am." That's the kind of content that makes most of us feel like trash—and hit unfollow.

So here's the reframe: flip "look at me" into "learn from me."

For example, instead of just posting a photo of myself on stage with a #blessed caption, I'll say something like, "Being a professional speaker is a dream, but I still get stage fright. Here are 3 things I do to calm my nerves before I present." Same photo. Same reminder of what I do. But now it's of service.

Promote your ideas. Share your art. Give people a takeaway. Let them walk away with something—insight, inspiration, value. This is how you stay top of mind and in alignment. Because if people can't see you, they can't hire you. If they don't know what you do, they can't refer you. And if you're too scared to show up, they'll find someone else who isn't.

Be visible. Be valuable. Be undeniable.

YOU
ARE
WHAT
THE
WORLD
NEEDS

if you
wan
na
get
what
you
reall
y
want,

then you've gotta be who you really are.

EDGE

Real talk? The truth about what's made me successful in life is simple: my enthusiasm.

Look—I'm not Einstein. My ideas aren't earth-shattering. I don't have a PhD. I don't teach robust systems. I don't roll with a research team. And no, I didn't go to an Ivy League school. I was mostly a C student.

But yo—I got straight A's in the school of good vibes.

And while I may not hold a fancy degree, I do hold a degree in dopeness. I've got street smarts. I've got stories. I've got scars and swagger. I've lived through enough pain and built enough resilience to give my words weight. And honestly? I think that's 90% of being successful in any business: your actual audacity. Maybe even a little Bambi-eyed delusion. That leaves 10% for the rest—strategy, structure, takeaways, and tactics.

And let's be real—every opportunity I've ever had came straight outta the struggle. Nothing's been handed to me. Nothing's come easy. Except this: my enthusiasm. Like, when I love something or believe in something or find something that's changed my life—I can barely help myself. I want to shout it from the rooftops.

For years, people mistook my enthusiasm for energy. And while they might look the same, they're not. I'm more introverted than most people think. I have to work hard to charge up my energy. But my enthusiasm? Oh my goodness—it's effortless. It's electric. When I love something, I go all in.

So instead of being embarrassed by it...
Instead of bowing down to the passive-aggressive "you're too much" crowd...
Instead of hiding this magic I possess...

I built a career out of it. I turned it into a magnetic speaking presence. It's my edge—in business, on stage, and in life. I'm enthusiastic. I own it. I love it. I'm grateful for it. Because my enthusiasm gives me energy—real, authentic, from-the-core energy. And that kind of energy? It gives other people permission to feel alive, too.

So what about you? You don't need to fake hype or be louder than you are. But you do need to know what lights you up. Want to find your edge? Start here: What could you talk about for hours—and never get tired of?

Your answer might just be the thing that sets you free.

I know I am
my grandmother's dream—
and so are you.
We are what our grandmothers fought for,
facing our fears,
feeling finally free.
the path they paved
is how all this came to be.
With a symphony of sisters beside them,
a world was built
where we could become the designers.
Now—
the architects of our own dreams,
we shape the future,
pave the path,
paint the picture
we want—
because we can.
Thanks to what they did.
So yeah, I was born to holler.
Words, my machete.
The mic, my flame.
Carving truth
into power and name.
Building legacy
by turning my life
into the ultimate high beam.
Becoming my own queen.
Living free,
no longer in between—
now fully seen.
A force supreme.
A Holler redeemed.

WHAT'S YOUR PARACHUTE?

There's a lot of "advice" out there disguised as wisdom—but some of it is just trash.

Case in point: "Just jump, and the net will catch you."

I can't even. It's so bad. Because let's be real—the only reason anyone jumps out of a plane in the first place is because they have a parachute on their back.

So let me ask you: What's your parachute?

For example, when I set out to become a professional keynote speaker, I didn't just peace out of my corporate job with a vision board and some palo santo. For three years, I tucked away money from every single paycheck. I saved, planned, and prepared. That savings became my parachute when I finally made the leap from Corporate America to full-time speaker. An aspirational quote didn't catch me. The money in my bank account did.

Whether you want to launch a business, leave a relationship, change careers, or chase your next dream, your preparation is what determines your success. Passion is essential, but a plan is non-negotiable. The pros don't "just jump." They build the net first.

So—what's the jump you're dreaming about? And what's in your parachute?

Maybe it's mentorship. Maybe it's savings. Maybe it's therapy, a side hustle, a coach, a five-year plan, or a folder full of ideas. Whatever it is, build it before you leap. That way, when you land, you won't just survive—you'll soar.

I spoke to my most high-profile audience yet—
thirty tween girls at a summer camp in Scottsdale.
If you want to test your skills as a presenter?
Speak to tweens.
They see through the bullshit.
They'll call you out.
And their faces will show you instantly
if you're a vibe—or not.
Thank God I brought disco balls—
a shimmering distraction
from the flavor of nerves
I was feeling
as I set out to inspire,
and help them keep dealing
with life as a tween—
especially when we all know
kids can be so mean.
Because see—
most of the work I create as an adult
is really made to heal lowercase Judi.
The little Judith in me,
Still searching.
Still growing.
So as I stood in front of the twenty tweens last week,
I flashed back to how I used to be:
Afraid to be seen,
Unsure of myself,
Definitely awkward,
Endlessly waiting for 12th.
But this was my moment—
to remind them of their power.
That they are queens in their tower.
And all of our broken pieces?
Actually perfectly in touch.
So I grab my shiny prop and proudly shout—
"You are a disco ball, baby!"
As they cheered in tandem—
the light of its mirrors
quickly becoming
our anthem.

TALENT

Rapper names are one of the boldest flexes on the planet. Seriously, have you ever stopped to think about the level of audacity it takes to crown yourself with a name like Talent? Yeah, I was listening to a Spotify playlist the other day, and I couldn't help but think, Damn, this dude just named himself Talent. No second-guessing. No false humility. Just pure, unadulterated confidence. He's out here like, "Yup, I'm Talent."

And it got me thinking—rappers just get it. They crown themselves with their greatness before anyone else does. They don't wait for permission. They don't play small. They just decide who they are, claim it loudly, and go hard in the paint proving it. And let me tell you, there's something so magnetic about that kind of audacity.

Some of my favorite rap names just scream confidence:

- Future – Imagine being so confident you just decide you ARE the future.
- Slick Rick – Smooth, confident, and way too cool to care what you think.
- LL Cool J – Ladies Love Cool James. Enough said.
- Ice Cube – Cold, unbothered, and always coming correct.
- Ludacris – Because why not just call yourself what you are—wild, bold, and a little bit crazy.
- Grandmaster Flash – Self-appointed legend status from day one.
- Qveen Herby – a literal queen spelling it her way and owning every inch of her power

Rappers don't wait for permission to be legendary—they just claim it and step into it. And I think we can borrow some belief from that. Because how often do we dim our light, talk ourselves down, or second-guess our worth because we're afraid of being seen as arrogant or "too much"?

Here's a wild thought: What if you stopped waiting for validation and just named yourself Greatness? What if you stepped into your dreams like you already owned them? What if, instead of worrying about being too audacious, you went even harder with it? The world needs more bold declarations and audacious moves. We've gotta stop playing small. You know who you are. You know what you're capable of. Own it, holler at your dreams, and make sure they know who's coming.

Her photo sits on my desk—
a daily reminder of legacy,
of roots,
and time's brutal truth.
Sparking a sense of urgency—
for expression,
and lessons,
becoming blessings,
Finally done second-guessing,
as I look to the heavens,
feeling her presence
in every second.

When you've lost your way,
when you don't know what to say—
when you fear getting it wrong,
when your dark night lasts a little too long...
Call on the muse.
She'll inspire you.
Guide you.
Hold you.
Mold you.
She'll bring you back home,
make you feel less alone,
pick you up like a phone,
get you back in the zone,
show you how you've grown,
prop you back up on your throne.
As she unveils the truth—
smooth as vermouth,
sweet like fruit—
that the muse
is
was
and always will be
YOU.

DON'T LISTEN

One of the most transformational choices I've ever made—sometimes boldly, sometimes with knees shaking like Bambi—was to not listen. Not to my best friend. Not to my brand manager. Not to my agent, my partner, my auntie, or the algorithm. Because my intuition knew better.

If I look back on the moves that lit the biggest fires in my life, they weren't born from someone else's blueprint. They came from inside—from that deep, undeniable knowing in my gut. The kind of truth you don't need to validate. You just feel it in your bones. Because if something doesn't belong to you, it won't stay with you. And you won't want to stay with it.

That's why I've learned to ignore advice that didn't resonate—even if it was well-meaning. Because the second you start creating so your friends will "get it"... or so your partner will approve... or so your family will be proud... you've already lost the magic. You're not creating from alignment—you're creating for applause.

Yes, let yourself be inspired. Yes, collaborate. But you have to be the main source of inspiration. Otherwise, you'll end up producing someone else's dream—and hating the results.

So please—don't water yourself down. Don't smooth your edges to be more "marketable." Don't take every note.

Trust your bones. Let your work reflect your joy. Make things that feel like home to you. Because when you do, the people who are meant for it will find it. They'll find you.

So love your people. But don't let them design your destiny. Their comfort is not your creative brief.

You're not here to make sense to everyone.
You're here to make something original.

MAKE IT
~~FAKE IT~~
'TIL YOU MAKE IT.

DOECHII WITH IT

There's a video of the pop-culture sensation Doechii that stopped me mid-scroll one day. She's sitting in front of her camera—raw and real, way before she got famous—saying something like: "I just lost my job. I have nothing to lose. So I'm going all in on my music. I'm gonna show up to every record store, production studio, and music space in town until someone lets me in."

She didn't wait for a label. Or a manager. Or a big break.
She became the break.

She independently released her mixtape Oh the Places You'll Go, featuring the viral "Yucky Blucky Fruitcake," and the rest? History. She went Doechii with it. Full creative control. Full voice. Full fire. She did it her way—and later got picked up by Top Dawg Entertainment and Capitol Records, on her own terms.

That video lit me up. Because when it came time to publish this book, I could've gone the traditional route. I had options. But this time? I wanted to do it my way. So I went Doechii with it.

I built my own team. I became the creative director. I stopped trying to get picked —and picked myself. Not because I couldn't get a deal. But because I didn't need one to make this magic real.

And I'm not the only one. Rupi Kaur—poet, performer, and powerhouse—is another one who went Doechii with it well before there was even a Doechii. She self-published milk and honey in 2014 with a pen, a vision, and zero permission. It became one of the best-selling poetry books of the 21st century—selling over six million copies, living on the New York Times bestseller list for four years straight.

In 2024, that book celebrated its 10-year anniversary with a collector's edition, a global fanbase, an Amazon Prime special, and more. All from a self-published start.

Proof. It's possible.

So if you've been waiting for permission?
Stop waiting.
Go Doechii with it.

Like a dark night
that sees the sunrise,
I should never have to dim my light—
because someone else
thinks it's too bright.

EIGHT

If you ever feel lost, stuck, or unsure of who the heck you are anymore… go hang out with your 8-year-old self. That's the real you. Before the world told you to be quiet, sit still, calm down, and blend in. Before you started shrinking to make other people comfortable. Before middle school came for your soul with braces, bullies, and bad cafeteria pizza.

Between the ages of birth and 7, our subconscious minds are sponging up every belief, behavior, and pattern in our environment—no filter, no boundaries. But somewhere between 8 and 10? That's when we start to become. Before we started dimming. Before we began doubting. Before life tells us to sit down and be a "good girl."

So, when I felt the call to reinvent recently, one of the first things I asked myself was, "Who was little Judi?" I started calling family, phoning the aunties, collecting stories of this wild, neon-loving, mic-holding, bubble-braided baby boss. She was a performer. A creator. A light. A force.

She still is.

That 8-year-old is my roadmap. So if you're lost, go there. Reconnect. Recall. Rewrite.

And if you're a parent of an 8-to-10-year-old right now? Keep a soul journal. Write down the songs they love. The outfits they insist on. The questions they ask. The weird-ass hobbies. One day they'll need a reminder of who they really are—and you'll be holding the key to their comeback story.

Because the most powerful version of you is already inside of you. And she's 8 years old waiting for you to call her home.

I will no longer shove down who I am.
See, I know
I'm like… bam!
A real goddess.
A fueled-up rocket.
A baller with deep pockets.
So I confidently take audits—
On my life,
Urgently cleaning up who's in my circle.
Feeling no envy.
Having no enemies.
Knowing adversaries are only here to enlighten me,
To inspire me.
Which makes me feel so free
To be who I was born to be.
So I'm calling my shot—
and HOLLERING at my dreams,
No longer afraid to be seen,
As I bob and weave,
through spaces once mean,
Turning pressure—into self-esteem.

BE THE TREND

I went to an all-girls high school, and in my graduating class of about 80 girls, everybody knew everybody. So when the senior yearbook came out—especially the back of the book with the Senior Superlatives—it was kind of a big deal. I was voted "Trendiest."

Kind of awesome.
Kind of cringe.
Kind of… still awesome.

I've always loved trends. I've followed them, worn them, let them inspire my vibe. But over the years—especially as an artist—that relationship has evolved. I still pay attention to what's trending in fashion, culture, music, and art. But I don't follow trends anymore. I remix them. I flip them. I set them.

One of the small ways I practice that is by refusing to ask, "What's everyone wearing?" Unless it's a wedding (no white—I'm bold, not evil) or a black-tie event (not showing up in sweats), I wear what my soul tells me to wear. Hoodie or haute couture—it depends on the energy. Because I don't dress to impress. I dress to express.

Style is just one place to practice this, but the truth is—everything in your life is a canvas. Your message. Your leadership. Your voice. Your work. So ask yourself: are you trying to match the room, or are you there to light it up?

Trendsetters don't ask what's safe. They lead with what's true. And the people who leave a mark? They don't chase what's hot—they embody what's real. So whether it's your outfit, your art, or your next big idea—stop waiting for consensus. Start trusting your creative instincts. That's your edge. And when you live from that place, everything you touch becomes iconic.

This isn't about a price tag. It's about presence. And the courage to show up like no one else can.

THE DOUBLE SELF COMBO

If I'm hiring someone—or choosing anyone to build with, collaborate with, or bet on—there are two things I'm always looking for: self-awareness and self-esteem.

Why? Because confident, self-aware people don't get caught up in petty drama, gossip, or office politics. I once heard Gary Vaynerchuk say it best in a scroll-stopping Instagram rant: self-aware people aren't sitting around obsessing over why Kathy in Accounting didn't say hi this morning or why David in Sales is getting more recognition than they are. They know who they are. They know what they do well. They stay in their lane and play their game. And they get that someone else's win isn't their loss—it's just proof that winning is possible.

Insecure people, on the other hand? They stir the pot. They crave validation. They energy vampire an environment. They create friction where there should be flow. That's why I believe one insecure employee can throw off an entire culture.

So if you want to build a better business, a better team, or a better life—hire for the "Double Self Combo": self-esteem and self-awareness.

Better yet, cultivate it. In yourself. In your people. Because when someone knows who they are—and who they're not—they naturally become more grounded, more confident, and way less concerned with what everyone else is doing. Which means: better results, stronger retention, and next-level resiliency.

I sway in the breeze,
roots deep and strong.
I bend, but never break—
held by a force
that's been there all along.

Mrs. Brown

Saw me—back in elementary. It's like she knew who I came to be before I knew anything about what God had in store for me. Which makes sense... I was only ten. Just a kid starting middle school. Fifth grade it was—when she handed me my first speech. A monologue to memorize for the upcoming speech meet. She signed me up to compete.

So with stars in my eyes, I took that script home, read it word for word—felt more alive with each verb that rolled off my tongue, out of my 10-year-old soul, from someplace deep in my bones.

I practiced my speech, getting ready to compete—not knowing at the time how this moment, this performance, would shape the rest of my life.

It was a sunny Saturday when I walked into Classroom 105. Thirty steel chairs lined in rows, full of strangers I didn't know—except for my dad, beaming in the front row. I took a deep breath, saw Mrs. Brown walking down the aisle. Her hand found my shoulder—"You're next," she whispered with a smile.
In minutes, I'd be up. Center stage. Sharing my memorized monologue to a room of strangers... like an entertainer.

Finally, it was time. I stepped to the mic, brushed back my hair, smoothed down my dress—to make sure it was just right. Oddly, I wasn't nervous. I felt at home. I grabbed the mic... and it all felt just right.

People stirred in their seats. Was that a laugh? Did that woman just wipe a tear? And then—thirty strangers stood to cheer. Mrs. Brown, proud and glowing. Me—on top of the world, floating.

I couldn't believe I did all that... with my tiny, 10-year-old soul. So when I left that room clutching gold in my hand, I finally began to understand who I am.

LIGHTNING MACHINE

My bags were packed and I was nonstop to LA, baybee! We landed safely and I jump off the plane at LAX with a dream ... and my shades still proudly on my face. My ego was so big, I don't know how it fit through the plane door but I was coming in hot, ready to hang with my peeps—fellow artists, poets, and performers who speak. At a conference called The Lightning Machine, created by mentor and muse, the POET and GOAT himself, Sekou Andrews.

Now, this trip was just for me. I was rolling solo. Time to roll deep—with myself, for myself, by myself. A weekend to tap into my talent, my voice. To honor the divine timing of my life. To address this tug I'd been having in my soul, deep down in my bones—that I was meant to use my spoken word. To be the verb I was born with. To wake up these gifts lying dormant. To finally stop waiting for an endorsement. It was time to pick me. I had to HOLLER at this dream—if only just to see.

So, my ego and me land in LA at 9:05 on a Friday morning and by 9 p.m. that same night, I was on the bathroom floor of my hotel room, in an iconic ugly cry. What am I doing here? I am so out of my league. Who do I think I am? I'm not unique. I should have started years ago. I am way too old. This is probably the end of the road. I should just go back to my comfort zone. So, I pick up the phone and call my husband back at home—ugly cry to him, start to feel a little less alone. Then I call my bestie, gave her the same ugly cry. Both of them reminding me how brave I am to try.

Eventually, I find the strength to stop my ugly cry. The clouds slowly begin to part in my self-induced dark sky. I pick myself up off the bathroom floor, place my hands on the counter, wipe a tear from my eye, let out a big sigh, look myself dead in the mirror, and begin my rally cry: HOLLER. Get yourself together. Do you know who you are? You are a star. An icon. A legend. You just signed up for a conference. Flew to L.A. to attend that conference. By yourself. For yourself. To learn. To grow. To tighten up your flow. You put yourself in the room. YOU ARE IN THE ROOM! That is brave. That is bold. Imposter Syndrome hasn't arrived—YOU have. Because if fear is here, you're doing it right. So I'm going to need you to get it together. Take a shower. Light a candle. Catch a vibe. And get some good sleep tonight. Because tomorrow, we ride. You will wake up, get up, dress up, and get yourself back in that room. Because you are about to bloom. MIC DROP. Boom.

And I did. I got myself together. I got myself back in that room, no longer consumed with fear, kicking myself into another gear—feeling open, deeply knowing that I wouldn't be here if something bigger wasn't the engineer.

That weekend in LA ended on a Sunday. So, I jumped back on a plane at LAX with a dream and a neon notebook full of ideas—my ego now with nowhere to go. Because I had found my way back home—to myself. Putting my fear, my pride, and my ego up on the shelf, stepping into something else, something even better: CONFIDENCE. And I found it at a conference called The Lightning Machine, created by a mentor and muse, Sekou Andrews, who taught me:

> **"MAYBE IT'S TIME TO STOP CHASING LIGHTNING AND START MAKING IT INSTEAD."**

Growth
shouldn't feel like
a life sentence
in solitary confinement.
But she feels so lonely,
constantly in refinement—
redefining,
trying to follow her assignment:
alignment.
So she stands tall
as she drops dead weight
like leaves in fall.
Feeling lighter.
Letting go
of those who don't like
the roots she's putting down—
deep into the ground.
Building strength
for the next bloom
in spring.
See, that's the thing
about growing.
You'll blossom.
They won't want you to.
But when you do—
they'll want your fruit,
even though they mock what you do.
But she knows she's a mirror
holding up a light
that blocks out the dark night
of anyone throwing shade
at her growth,
unafraid.
Because with each leaf that drops,
she plants seeds—
for a future that feeds
her own design.
Because she's not here to shrink—
she's here to align.

YOU DON'T NEED PERMISSION.
YOU NEED A MIRROR—
AND A MATCH.

SOUL OF A SELF-STARTER

No one handed me a six-figure book deal. No one crowned me a poet. No one told me, "We've been waiting for your art." I had to anoint myself. I had to crown myself. I created—and claimed—my own book deal. I had to say it out loud: I'm a poet. I'm an artist. I'm a writer. And I'm self-publishing this book now, on my terms, because I can no longer not.

I didn't wait to be picked. I picked myself. I built my own team. I made my own lane. I built my own house—and painted the door pink.

Meanwhile, most people are still sitting quietly, politely, waiting to be discovered.

Following the rules. Shrinking their desires. Trying not to be too much. Hoping someone notices their potential before they're ready to claim it themselves. That's the danger of conditioning: it teaches you to wait. To be liked. To be safe. To keep your hands folded while your soul screams for more.

But here's the truth: no one's coming. Not with permission. Not with a map. Not with the perfect invitation. Creating your own opportunity isn't about being loud. It's about being brave. It's about starting before you feel ready. Betting on yourself when there's no applause. Following the breadcrumbs with no recipe. And moving faster—while being less perfect.

You don't need someone else's crown. You need to recognize your own reflection. So build the thing. Pitch the thing. Write the thing. Start the thing. Your very existence is the green light. And your dreams? They've been waiting on you.

If you want to build confidence, go where you have none **on purpose, regularly.**

OWN THE MOMENT

I was recently booked by a client in the live events space, and during our prep call, they walked me through their brand's DNA—an ethos rooted in owning every moment. How dope is that?

As they unpacked their strategy, strand by strand, it hit me: this exercise isn't just powerful for brands—it's essential for anyone building something meaningful. A business. A message. A life. Because clarity? Clarity is magnetic.

When you know who you are and what you stand for, everything else gets easier—sales, storytelling, decision-making, even what you post online. You stop chasing. You start attracting.

So here's a challenge for you. Whether you're running a business or running your life like a CEO, grab a notebook and ask yourself:

1. What's your vision?
    - Where are you going—and why does it matter?
2. What's your mission?
    - What are you here to do—and how will you do it?
3. What are your values?
    - What's non-negotiable? What guides your decisions?
4. What makes you different?
    - What's your edge? Your soul stamp? Your POV?
5. What's your brand personality?
    - If your brand were a person, how would it move, speak, dress, and show up?

Once your answers feel real and aligned, let them drive everything—your content, your copy, your elevator pitch, your team meetings, your offers, your yeses, and your awwwwww, hell no's. Let this become your inner compass. Your clarity code. Your strategy, story, and soul—all in one.

She stares at the snake
and the slow way it moves,
feeling jealous of the time it takes her
to glide between the grooves.
No rush.
No race.
Just pace—
as she winds her way
through the desert landscape.
Now suddenly finding herself desiring
to be more like this snake—
long,
lean,
slow,
steady,
venom on the ready.
Fierce when provoked,
but peaceful inside,
an ancient grace
she no longer hides.
Shedding skin
to become what's true,
leaving behind
what no longer grew.
Embracing the wild,
the instinct, the drive—
the quiet, untamed
need to survive.

ORIGINALITY

Let's take some big pressure off your shoulders: nothing is truly original. And that's not a diss—it's a liberation.

I was listening to one of my favorite graffiti artists, Futura, back this up by sharing that his "tag name" has been attached to vacuums, cars, and blenders. Literally. There's a Ford Futura, a Hoover Futura, a Braun Futura. He joked about how his name wasn't "original" on paper—and he's right. But the way he writes it, the way he makes it move, the way he became it? That's what makes it original.

Because originality isn't about being the first.
It's about being real.

Everything we create—everything—is shaped by what we take in. The books we read. The music we blast. The cities we visit. The friends we love. The fears we've faced. The things we've lost. The things we've dreamed. All of it remixes inside of us and becomes something new. Not because it's never been done—but because we're the ones doing it.

You're the remix.
You're the perspective.
You're the art.

Think of a museum. The art doesn't come alive until someone's standing in front of it. A painting without a viewer is just pigment on canvas. It's the presence of a person—their interpretation, their energy, their soul—that makes it feel alive.

Same goes for your ideas, your art, your expression. The soul behind it is what makes it matter.

So if you're paralyzed by the pressure to be original, let it go. You don't have to invent something brand new. You just have to show up in it fully. Make it yours. Put your name on it, your voice in it, your lens through it. That's what makes something original. Not because it's new—but because it's true.

HAPPILY EVER NOW.

YOUR JOB IS FUN

I love Dave Chappelle. Hands down, one of my favorite comedians of all time. Recently, I heard him tell a story about a fan who came up to him and said, "Man, your job is so fun."

Dave replied: "No, man. My job isn't fun. My job is a job. I'm fun."

Funny AND real AF.

Why do I love it so much? Well, because it's such a simple but powerful reminder that fun isn't about what you do—it's about how you be.

Even as a stand-up comic—whose literal job is to make people laugh—it's still work. There's pressure. Deadlines. Stress. Expectations. Failure. Criticism. The job itself? Not always fun. But he is. That's his power. That's his choice.

And guess what? You've got that same power.

You don't have to be a comedian to bring joy. You don't need a cool job title to have a good time. Whether you're an accountant, a speaker, a teacher, a barista, or building your own empire—your job is a job. The fun part? That's you. That's how you choose to show up.

You're in the driver's seat. You decide how much pressure to pile on. You decide how seriously you take yourself. You decide if you're going to walk into that meeting like a chore—or like a vibe.

Fun isn't the function of your work. It's the expression of your spirit. So don't wait for a title, a team, or a new career to feel more alive.

Be the fun.

Because when you are—you shift the whole room. And suddenly, the job starts to feel different. Because you do.

Despite everything
that tried to undo her,
she arrived anyway—
undone.
unstoppable.
unbothered.

REPEL TO ATTRACT

I talk a lot about getting to know yourself—what you want, what you believe in, what sets your soul on fire. And yes, that's crucial. But here's the other half of the equation: it's just as important to know what you don't want.

Clarity isn't just about defining your desires—it's about cutting away everything that doesn't align. It's knowing what you won't tolerate. Who you aren't for. What no longer deserves your time, energy, or explanation.

When I rebranded my business and returned home to HOLLER, rooting my message in the verb I was born with, I got crystal clear on what I did want. But just as important? I got brutally honest about what I didn't.

The clients who drained me. The speaking gigs that didn't feel aligned. The parts of my business that made me feel like I couldn't breathe. And most of all—the outdated, people-pleasing version of me that kept shrinking to make others comfortable.

For too long, I contorted myself into a version I thought would be more "palatable." I said yes when I meant hell no. I dulled my edge to avoid making waves. I played it safe. But here's the truth: Playing it safe is just slow-motion self-abandonment.

And if you're constantly trying to make everyone happy, you'll always be at war with yourself.

You are not for everyone. And you're not supposed to be.

When you stop chasing approval and start standing fully in who you are, something radical happens. The wrong people fall away. The right people find you. Alignment clicks. Energy returns. Business gets lighter. Life gets louder.

So get wildly clear on what's not for you. And don't waste one ounce of your energy apologizing for it.

Because when you start repelling the wrong things, you finally make space to attract the right ones. And that's when the real magic begins.

I'M INTUITIVE.
I SEE FAKE PEOPLE.

slowly
surely
sweetly
she moves
intentionally
intuitively
taking a beat
feeling the breeze
pinch me, please
she thinks
as she pulls back from rushing
almost blushing
at the pleasure she feels
from doing nothing
simply
and
seductively
becoming

SEQUIN SKIRT

"OK, this is bullshit," my best friend said, yanking the sequin skirt out of the pile. "You love that skirt. It's your book launch skirt. I'm sorry, but that is going back in your closet!"

She wasn't playing. One by one, she pulled out more things I'd been told to get rid of—things that were "no longer allowed" because they were "not my vibe" anymore. Every time she put something back on the hanger, I felt relief wash over me. I've never been more grateful to call her my best friend—someone who sees me, knows me, and calls bullshit on my bullshit when I lose my way and veer too far from home base.

See, there's a profound shift that happens the moment you try to fit in: You abandon parts of yourself. It might be subtle at first—a tweak in how you dress, a bite of your tongue in a conversation, or a laugh that feels slightly forced. But over time, these small compromises erode the authentic parts of who you are. You start questioning your choices, second-guessing your instincts, and feeling like you need permission to just be you.

The moment you try to fit in, you send a subconscious message to yourself: Who I am is not enough.

That's a dangerous lie. A lie we tell ourselves when we prioritize external validation over internal truth. When we believe we must conform to succeed, to be liked, or to be loved.

So the next time you feel yourself abandoning the parts that make you, YOU, remember that what got you here is the whole reason you're going there. You don't have to trade your soul for success. You don't have to give away your power to fit into someone else's mold. Elevate, evolve, grow—but take the best of you with you.

Because the right people? They'll love the real you, sequin skirts and all

FEARLESS. SELF EXPRESS.

If you still don't see me
when I'm fully being me,
then you are not for me—
so free, I will set me.

YOU ARE THE POWERPOINT

One thing I've always believed to my core as a presenter: slides are not the show—you are. Yes, a well-designed deck can be a beautiful, artistic expression. A vibe. A visual punctuation mark. But slides are a supporting cast member, not the lead. They're there to enhance your story, not deliver it for you.

Unless you're a researcher, doctor, or academic delivering complex data, your slides should function like a bold exclamation point. Something that punctuates the message. Something visually interesting that helps guide the story—not hijack it.

Because at the end of the day? You are the PowerPoint.

Your stories.
Your energy.
Your wisdom.
Your voice.
The way you move.
The way you are simply because you exist.

That's the real presentation. That's what shifts the frequency in a ballroom. That's what turns a convention center into a living, breathing, electric machine. Not the slides—but the soul delivering them.

Let your deck throw confetti, not steal the mic.

So whether you're a keynote speaker or just pitching your next big idea, here's your challenge: Reimagine your next presentation. Let the slides back you up—but never let them take your spotlight.

You are the experience.

Own it like it was designed just for you—because it was.

Like a fern
I flow
With the breeze
At ease
The peace
Bringing me to my knees
Slowly curing this disease
of rushing 'til I sleep—
a pace I never chose,
but forgot I could leave.

VAN DOWN BY THE RIVER

For a long time, I was low-key mortified to be called a motivational speaker. Anytime my husband or friends introduced me that way, it felt like nails on a chalkboard. Thick. Cringe. You might as well have told people I lived in a van down by the river (Chris Farley, SNL Sketch, 1994—if you know, you know).

Then, one night, sitting on our front porch in Ohio, I was venting to my husband and stepson, Sam, about this full-blown identity crisis. I went off: "Maybe I'm a Chief Energy Officer? A Motivational Raptress? An Artist? A Creative Entrepreneur?" I was desperate to call myself anything but a motivational speaker.

Sam, who was in med school at the time, stopped me mid-rant and said, "Judi, did you know only 20% of med students become surgeons?"

I shook my head no.

Sam went on: "And did you also know that 80% of people would rather die than speak in public?"

I nodded yes.

Then he said, "You're basically a surgeon. You do something 80% of people are terrified of. And to be able to motivate people while you do it? Icing on the cake." Mic. Drop. Then, I immediately Googled the word motivation.

Motivation: The reason or willingness to act or behave in a particular way. The desire to do something.

The title I'd been running from? It was an honor. From that moment on, I owned it. Because once I let go of the shame and leaned all the way into my niche, I took bolder action and found my people.

So now I ask you: What title, belief, or identity are you afraid to claim? Who told you it wasn't "cool enough"? What would happen if you stopped running from it—and stood in it instead? Here's the truth: most of the things that hold us back are self-imposed. And the minute you finally claim your space? You become unstoppable.

Like a record needle on the edge,
she dances along life's cutting ledge.
With every step, she finds her groove—
confidence building, making moves.

She scratches doubt, remixes fear,
drops big beats, like desert heat.
She spins past limits, and sets the tone—
not just surviving—she's in the zone.

HONEST SIGNALS

Before you say a word, the room already knows. Your energy walked in first.

That's the power of honest signals—a real concept coined by MIT professor Alex Pentland in his book Honest Signals: How They Shape Our World. His research shows that we are constantly communicating through subconscious, nonverbal cues—tone, gesture, timing, posture—long before we ever speak. Your vibe either says, "I'm safe," or "something's off." And it all happens in a split-second.

"Honest signals are the invisible forces—tone, timing, micro-movements—that shape how we connect long before words ever enter the chat."
—Based on the research of MIT's Alex Pentland, Honest Signals

This is why some people feel magnetic the moment you meet them. Their energy is clean. Aligned. Honest. There's no gap between who they are and who they're being. And that kind of congruence? It's felt. You trust it immediately.

But this is also why certain people feel… off. You can't always put your finger on it, but your body knows. Your stomach tightens. Something in you recoils. There's a gap between the performance and the truth—and that gap creates discomfort, even creepiness. This is why wax figures feel weird. No honest signals. No life. Just mimicry. Same thing happens with filtered personas on social media. That's why they feel fake. Because they are.

You're transmitting honest signals all day long—and so is everyone else. Which means one of the most powerful things you can do is get better at reading them—and trusting what you read. Especially when it comes to relationships, hiring, and partnerships. Your body will tell you. Listen to the first feeling, not the fallout.

We've all ignored honest signals and paid the price. Gotten too close to people we knew were off. Hired someone we felt weird about. Dated someone our gut flagged. And when it implodes, we say the same thing: "Shit. I knew it."

I've had that happen more than once. But not anymore. These days, I don't play with energy vampires. If you suck the life out of the room, I don't care how charming or qualified you are—you're not for me. I've got grace for family dynamics, and yes, boundaries can help in those cases. But when it comes to friends or team members? I'm cutthroat. Life's too short. Peace is too expensive.

So if something feels off—it probably is. That's your body reading someone's honest signals before your brain catches up. Believe it.

SOUL > SCROLL

LESS SCROLLING,
MORE SOULING.

THE ALGORITHM IS YOU THE ALGORITHM IS YOU THE ALGORITHM IS YOU THE ALGORITHM IS YOU

SOUL > BRAIN

Here's the thing about our big, beautiful brains: they're doing their job. And their job is survival. So before I go any further, let me be clear—I'm not hating on the brain. It is a miracle. A master of protection. A vault of memory. A quick-fire analyst, always calculating risk and reward, always scanning for danger. And wow—is it good at its job.

So good, in fact, that if we're not careful, it can become a problem. Because the brain's job is to protect us in the present by pulling from the past. That means it's always cross-referencing what happened before: past failure, past rejection, past humiliation, past hurt. It's like an internal risk manager whispering, "You tried that once and got burned—let's not do that again." Or, "Remember when you spoke up and they gave you that look? Stay quiet this time." Or maybe, "Don't be too much. Don't take up space. Just play it safe."

But the soul? The soul doesn't care about playing it safe. The soul is your future's GPS. It knows who you are, who you're becoming, and what you came here to do.

The problem is, the brain is louder. Faster. More practiced.

The soul is quieter. Wiser. But you've got to lean in to hear it. And now—more than ever—is the time to tune in. To make the bold choice not just to hear your soul, but to trust it.

Because the future won't be built by people who stay safely rooted in the past. It will be built by those willing to let intuition lead.

Invocation—

I honor you, my big, beautiful brain.
Thank you for keeping me safe.
I know you're doing your job, and I ask that you continue to do it well.
But today, I'm listening to my soul.
I'm letting my intuition speak.
And I'm choosing to move not from fear—but from faith.
Because my future depends on it.
And my soul already knows the way.

IDEA DJ

I've been thinking a lot about originality—and how many people are afraid to create because they're afraid of what people will say. That they're copying. That it's been done before. That someone else said it better. And yeah, in today's world, the minute you share something true, someone on the internet is ready to call it cringe or claim it as theirs.

But here's the thing: nothing is really original. Everything is borrowed from the universe. Everything we make is shaped by what we've lived, read, heard, seen, and survived. That doesn't make it less creative—it makes it more real.

We are all DJs. Idea DJs. We're here to spin what we've been given, sample what inspires us, and remix it into something only we can make. This book is my album. A mixtape of everything I've learned, lived, and loved. A body of work built on wisdom that's been swirling through me for years. I didn't steal it—I alchemized it.

So if you're out there holding back your truth, worried someone's going to say it's not original or roll their eyes or try to tear you down—I hope you remember this: they don't hate you. They hate that they're not expressing. Keep creating anyway. They'll talk regardless. Let 'em.

You're not here to be the first.
You're here to be the realest.

THE
THE SEA
THE SEA OF
THE SEA OF SAMENESS
THE SEA OF SAMENESS AIN'T
THE SEA OF SAMENESS AIN'T THAT
THE SEA OF SAMENESS AIN'T THAT DEEP.

COLOR THEORY FOR SOUL

You are the art. Not just the observer—the masterpiece in motion. And like any bold work of art, your presence is made of layers. Brushstrokes. Color. Mood. Energy. I've always been drawn to pop art—its vibrancy, its edge, its fearless refusal to blend in. What I love most is how it makes you feel. Because color isn't just something we see—it's something we experience. It evokes. It activates. It speaks before we do.

This next exercise is about tapping into that energy. Your inner pop is your emotional palette—your truth in full color. These prompts are designed to help you access it. Whether you write, paint, dance, or simply reflect, let each shade lead you deeper into the masterpiece of you.

Red: What's something you're fired up about right now? What makes your pulse quicken? Where in your life are you hungry for change, justice, or forward motion? Red is your rage, your passion, your power. It lives in your roar.

Pink: Where does your softness meet your strength? What makes you feel electric in your skin—unapologetically feminine, and undeniably in charge? Pink is more than cute. It's a stance. It's protest in a pretty shade. It's walking into the room and owning it without raising your voice. Pink is power—reclaimed, remixed, and worn like armor.

Yellow: Where does your joy live? What makes you laugh out loud, lose time, or feel lit from within? Yellow is your sunshine. Your truth. Your fearless light.

Green: What are you growing right now—internally or externally? What feels fresh, tender, or in progress? Green is your breath, your healing, your "I'm becoming" energy.

Blue: What truth have you been holding back? What needs to be said, sung, written, or whispered to the world—or to yourself? Blue is your voice. Your stillness. Your deep-end wisdom.

Purple: Where's your magic? What makes you feel rare, regal, and deeply you? Purple is your mystery. Your imagination. Your unshakable knowing.

Black (or Mixed Media): What mess have you moved through? What pain have you turned into poetry? Black is your depth. Your contrast. Your unapologetic edge.

Choose the color that calls to you. Let it lead you somewhere honest. Somewhere wildly dope. Somewhere real.

I got in his car,
felt his vibe like a beat—
a magnetic rhythm
that pulled me deeper into the seat.

He said, "I make music—
   it saved my life.
   I want to heal the world
   with sound, not fight."

"But I'm not trained," he added,
"no strings, no keys…"

I smiled and said,
   "Brother, please—

the instrument is you.

   Your soul: the melody of proof.
   The hum of healing.
   No sheet music needed.
   No formal degree.

   You are the sound.
                You are the frequency."

CRACKER BARREL

I hit 10K on Instagram in a Cracker Barrel bathroom. True story.

I was driving to Indy to visit my best friend for her birthday and pulled off at a Cracker Barrel for a rest stop—because let's be honest, I'd rather brave a Cracker Barrel restroom than a grimy gas station any day. Plus, I can never resist grabbing one of their homemade apple pie candles.

So there I was, in the stall, scrolling my phone (as we do), opening Instagram (as we do), and nearly dropping it in the toilet when I saw it—I had officially hit 10,000 followers. I squealed, ran to my car, and immediately called my biz besties. Back then, hitting 10K meant unlocking social media perks like the swipe-up feature (RIP), tagging stores, linking in stories, and, of course, gaining some serious street cred.

Yo, I felt so official.

That weekend, I walked around Indy like a celeb, half-expecting someone to stop me for an autograph. But a few weeks later, something shifted. I started obsessing over 20K. Then 30K. Then 50K. No number ever felt like enough.

Maybe for you, it's not followers. Maybe it's shoes, money, labels, the number on a scale, a bestseller list, or the inner circle you're still trying to break into. Whatever it is, let me hit you with this truth: if you want to slam headfirst into a brick wall in life and business, start bowing at the altar of false gods. The algorithm. The applause. The approval of strangers.

Striving for greatness is good—but you don't need strangers in a Meta boardroom to verify you.

You are verified because you were born.

HOLLER BACK

People hear my last name and assume hollering means being loud. But hollering isn't about volume—it's about vibe. It's not about noise. It's about knowing. It's not about shouting. It's about showing up.

Hollering is what happens when you're so aligned with who you are and where you're going, the world can't help but take notice—even if you never raise your voice. It's movement. It's action. It's the daily decision to bet on yourself by making one brave move at a time in the direction of your dreams.

Most of us don't have a plans problem—we have an action problem. It's easy to make a plan. It's harder to make a move. That's why most people don't.

But those of us who holler? We get it. We know it's not about being the loudest in the room—it's about being the realest. We're not yelling—we're aligning. We're not forcing—we're flowing.

Because we know the real secret: you will never get in this life what you aren't brave enough to holler at.

She was built to wait—
for the invitation,
for the recognition,
for the soft yes
that needs no permission.
Born with a verb,
a mission stitched on her chest,
she often felt misplaced
in a world obsessed with next.
But her power is patience.
Her magic? Pace.
She doesn't chase—
she holds the space.
She is soft.
She is steady.
She waits—
knowing she was born ready.
Joy, her compass.
Clarity, her flame.
She honors her timing—
and her name.
Her stillness isn't lack,
it's a sacred track
where the magic circles back—
to the last name
she's proud to have,
so she calls it back.

THE BULLPEN

In 2022, I got the kind of call that changes things. A friend—who just so happened to be the CEO of a big name company at the time—called to let me know one of their keynote speakers had come down with COVID. Their biggest event of the year was in three days, and they needed a pinch hitter. "Can you be there?" he asked.

The catch? I had to present in 72 hours. No slides. No improv with volunteers (my signature!). A tight 30-minute window. A small studio audience… but over 40,000 people tuning in when the talk aired.

The stakes were high, but my vibe was higher. I said yes.

That night, I went to bed with nerves buzzing and my soul stirring. At 3:00 AM, I shot up in bed. Something bigger than me poured through. Within an hour, I had the outline of a talk about regret—and the three questions I ask myself to avoid it. I rehearsed like hell, packed my favorite sequin suit, and flew to Cincinnati.

When I arrived, there it was: a giant disco ball hovering above the main stage—a glittering wink from the universe that I was right where I needed to be.

I gave the talk. And the next day, this email hit my inbox:
"Thank you for 'yes, and-ing.' I was bummed when [insert high profile confidential celeb speaker who came down with the VID here] couldn't make it. But you took our disappointment and spun it into something magical."

Here's the real moral of the story: life is improv. And luck? It's a skill. You don't get lucky without preparation. And preparation only matters if you're open to the unexpected. This was a big moment for me—not just professionally, but personally. It was the first time I gave a formal keynote without slides, without improv, without my usual go-tos. It forced me to trust that my stories, my voice, and my style were enough. Spoiler alert: they were. And so are yours.

So if the bullpen calls and your name is up—step up to the plate. Trust yourself. And take a swing. Because brave always beats safe. Every time.

Like a cheetah,
she moves with precision—
silent, certain, steady.
Unapologetically swift in her pursuit,
courage her machete,
hesitation her true predator—
and she'll never let it get ahead of her.

She eats disruption for breakfast,
hunts down discomfort for dinner,
licks her paws with pride—
a belly full of both,
knowing they make the best fuel
for ultimate growth.

She trusts her instincts,
feels the wind against her face—
letting momentum
be the roar
that sets her pace.

She doesn't chase to chase—
she chases to claim.
Because when instinct leads,
the wild obey,

EXPRESS TO BECOME

We hear it all the time: start before you're ready. But what about expressing before you're ready?

Most people stay silent until they feel perfectly polished—until their voice shakes less, until their ideas are fully formed and market-tested. And because of that? They miss the moment. They stay invisible. They sit on the sidelines of conversations they belong in, waiting for some imaginary "right" time that never shows up.

I learned to never wait for the luxury of being perfectly ready—because it doesn't exist. And I came to understand that if I waited for the luxury of readiness, I'd probably be waiting for the rest of my life.

Here's how that looked in real life: When I was in corporate, I learned how to express while I was still figuring it out. I'd challenge myself to be the first to ask a question on a conference call. I'd raise my hand early in a meeting—even if I wasn't sure my comment would be profound. Why? Because energy speaks. Initiative matters.

People remember the ones who have the courage to go first.

And guess what? It worked. I built visibility. Confidence. A reputation. Not because I had all the answers—but because I showed up with energy and effort.

I've done the same as a professional speaker. Looking back at some of my earliest talks? Cringe. But also? Proud. Because I said yes before I was polished. I expressed before I felt ready. And in doing that, I became who I was meant to be.

That's the thing: expression is how you become—not how you prove.
You don't speak because you're the smartest person in the room.
You speak because you're brave enough to be seen growing in real time.

So here's the move:
Express to become, not impress.
Raise your hand. Ask the question. Contribute. Take initiative.
Even if it's not perfect.
Especially then.

Because confidence doesn't come before the expression—
it's built inside of it.

I am the source.

I am the search bar, the spark, the flame—
the library, the download, the upload, the reload,
the reset, the blueprint, the AI—
because I am I.

I am. I am. I am.

SO, WHAT INSPIRES YOU?

In 2022, when we were searching for homes in Arizona and preparing to move across the country, a guy giving us a golf cart tour turned to me and casually asked, "That's so cool that you're an author and speaker—tell me, what inspires your work?"

Yo. Bruh. What.

My brain glitched—like a CD skipping. Like Wi-Fi in a storm. I fumbled out a string of nonsense, and as my hot mess express tried to recover, I watched his eyes glaze over. In ten seconds flat, I went from feeling cool… to level-10 cringe.

His question hit me hard—not because I didn't have inspiration, but because I couldn't name it. I hadn't taken the time to know what moves me. And if you're an artist, a creator, a communicator, or a human trying to live awake, inspiration isn't optional. It's your lifeline. Inspiration is how we stay present. It's how we co-create with the world instead of just reacting to it. And if you don't know what's inspiring you right now, chances are… you're not really creating. You're just consuming. You're scrolling, not seeing. You're reacting, not leading. You're plugged into the matrix more than your mission.

So, I vowed to never get caught off guard like that again. I started keeping a list—a living document in my Notes app labeled simply: People, Places, and Things That Inspire Me.

It's not for likes. It's not for anyone else. It's for me—to remember who I'm becoming and what energy I'm allowing to shape that becoming.

This question has also become my favorite icebreaker at networking events. We can small talk all we want—but it's questions like this that tell me the essence of someone's being. I don't get the corporate mask. I get their soul.
So if I were to meet you at a cocktail party and ask, What inspires you?—what would you say?

And if you don't have an answer yet, maybe today's the day you start your own Inspired By list. Keep it close. Keep it current. Add to it. Take things away. Let it evolve with you—your breadcrumb trail back to yourself. The spark that keeps you lit when things get dim.

PLAYING IT SAFE IS JUST SLOW-

MOTION
SELF-ABANDONMENT.

THE ART OF LETTING GO

Letting go isn't weak. It's not quitting. It's an art form—and one of the most powerful moves you'll ever master.

Over the last few years, I've had to let go of a lot: the version of success I thought I'd have, friendships I've outgrown, rooms I no longer fit into, speeches I spent years building that just aren't mine anymore, even clothes I once loved but don't feel like "me" now. Every one of those things was part of an older version of me—but none of them belonged to the woman I'm becoming.

Here's how I've learned to know it's time: if it's stealing my peace, it's gotta go. If it feels heavy when I talk about it, that's data. If I find myself fantasizing about something else, I listen. And if I'm only staying because I'm scared, I call that what it is—stuck, not aligned.

Letting go still stings. There's grief in the process. I've cried over relationship exits, creative projects, and curated outfits that just didn't feel like home anymore. But I've also learned this: peace is always waiting on the other side of release. When you stop forcing what no longer fits, something new always rushes in to take its place.

We don't talk about this enough, but outgrowing people, plans, and patterns is a spiritual practice. It requires trust. Trust in your timing, your truth, your next evolution.

So if you're wondering whether it's time to let something go, you probably already know the answer. Your body knows. The tension doesn't lie. You don't need another sign—you need to trust yourself.

CALL IT BACK

Anytime you accidentally give away your power, you can call it back. At any time. No questions asked. No shame needed. Power isn't a one-shot deal. You don't run out. You just forget you're the one holding it.

I know because it happened to me—with this book. Specifically, the title and the cover. It was time to make a final decision and I just… couldn't. I was pacing the hallways of my head, completely rattled. I couldn't sleep. I was snapping at my husband. I was breaking out like a teenager during finals week. Nothing felt right. We redesigned the cover. Again. And again. Still—it wasn't hitting. It wasn't giving. Something was off.

And then it hit me: I couldn't choose the cover because it wasn't mine. The title had been handed to me by a brand manager who (with good intentions) told me that a certain tagline would make me more "marketable" in corporate America. And because I was in a vulnerable place at the time—confused, unhealed, doubting myself—I let it happen. I said yes when I meant no way. I let outside voices get louder than my inner one. I was asking too many people for opinions and losing my own in the process.

When I first launched Holler at Your Dreams, I was unsteady. I put it out there, and it didn't land right away. And when someone snarked, "Well, how's that working out for you?"—I flinched. Instead of trusting the vision, I caved. I changed the title. The cover. The tone. Everything. I tried to make it all more palatable. More polished. More "marketable." And it still didn't work. Why? Because it wasn't mine.

It took me two years to realize the truth: If something is not yours, it won't stay with you. And you won't want to stay with it!

So I called it all back. My voice. My title. My truth. My creative vision. I pissed a few people off. And I came all the way out of the creative closet. No apologies. No turning back. That's why you're holding Holler at Your Dreams right now. Because I listened. Because I stopped performing and started remembering. Because I finally trusted the version of me that had always known. And I said the words out loud: This is mine.

So if you've lost your voice—or your vibe—or your vision—because you tried to be someone else for a while… call it back. You're allowed to change your mind. You're allowed to try again. You're allowed to be wrong, then get it right.

If I can see it,
I can have it.
And if I can have it,
it's already mine.

i am ready for all the BIG, JUICY, MAGICAL, ICONIC, DOPE opportunities coming my way.

THE PARADIGM

"WHEN YOU CHANGE THE RULES, ESPECIALLY WHEN NO ONE ELSE KNOWS THAT YOU HAVE, THE WORLD IS YOURS."
KEN BLACK

(TRANSCEND IT)

This is the leap. The moment we stop asking for permission and start rewriting the script. The paradigm isn't about fitting in—it's about rising above. It's where we take everything we've learned —through pain, through peace, through presence—and use it to step into an entirely new way of being.

We are no longer bound by the limitations we once accepted. No longer playing small in systems that were never built for us. Here, we define the game, break the mold, and move beyond the expected.

In this section, we ascend. We shift from playing within the rules to becoming the architect of our own reality. We stop living as a reaction to the world and start shaping the world with our very existence.

This is where we soar.

She is a soul in ascension.
She is the truth—not the tension.
She is the voice beyond convention.
She is her own divine invention.
She is the shift—the soul's intention.
She is the flame of new dimension.
She is the light past comprehension.
She is the pulse of reinvention.
She is the dreamer with divine retention.
She is her own full-body blessing.

SHE ALREADY IS

We spend so much time searching. Scrolling. Comparing. Looking for signs, titles, accolades, approval. But what if you already are? What if she already is? That woman you're chasing—the one who's more confident, clear, vibrant, fulfilled—what if she's not out there in the algorithm or waiting at the next milestone… but buried right beneath your nose?

I mean that literally.

Take my last name. Holler. I've had it my whole life. And it's always fit me. But for years, I missed the assignment. I didn't see the message because I was too busy living in other people's expectations, taking on their opinions, and trying to do things "the right way." I had this wildly original, soul-aligned clue hiding in plain sight—and it took me over 45 years to wake it up. To stop trying to fit in and start letting my truth lead.

Because Holler isn't about being loud. It's about being full. Fully expressed. Fully embodied. Fully alive. It's the enthusiastic transmission of who you are. And that's been in me all along.

So what's in you? What part of your DNA, your name, your past, your quirks, your truth have you been overlooking? What gifts are lying dormant, waiting for you to remember?

You don't have to become her. You just have to remember:

She's already here.
She already knows.
She already is.

I STAND LIKE A PYRAMID— A TIMELESS MYSTERY, BUILDING MY LEGACY, CRAFTING HISTORY.

Between the lines of life
and the heartbeat of dreams,
there's a city street stretch—
stitched in neon-lit seams,
where destiny's sketched,
potential untapped,
as she minds the gap—
between who she once was
and who she's becoming,
intuition now her only map.
No longer trapped,
confidence curled up in her lap,
she makes moves like a cat—
smooth like a last dance,
never looking back.
There's no time for that.
She must mind the gap,
and holler back.

BECOMING

My phone pings. It's a message from a friend and colleague I deeply respect, sharing one of those Apple-generated iPhone memories. A video montage from early 2023—the early days of us working together. I'm holding a massive disco ball, wrapped in a hot pink sequined suit, being photographed for a local magazine feature about an entrepreneurial award I'd just won.

Old Judi would've cringed. I would've texted back "Ick!" or sent a string of skull emojis to signify how mortified I was by my own audacity. But this time, I didn't. I just replied: "I love her. The beginning of the becoming." Because it was.

I was in the thick of transformation—heart cracked open, navigating deep pain, but also feeling an unshakable sense of trust. I didn't have the words for it then. I couldn't fully explain it. But I knew. I knew something bigger was unfolding. I was following the clues: the disco balls, the sequin suits, the people walking into my life, the strange and sparkly opportunities arriving on cue. I was being asked to trust the yes's and the no's. To believe the closed doors were divine protection. I remember feeling equal parts terrified and electric during that photo shoot—thrilled by the potential, haunted by the unknown.

But here's what I now understand: If fear is near, it means you're getting close. It means you're either being protected from something that's not for you, or you're about to rise into something wildly new. When you're stepping into territory you've never entered before, it will feel awkward, unfamiliar, and wildly uncomfortable—because you've never been there. You're not supposed to know what you're doing. That's not a red flag. That's the clue. Fear is not failure. It's the compass. It's a sign you're aligned, expanding, putting yourself out there. You're not hiding. You're not hedging. You're betting on yourself. You're hollering at your motherf*cking dreams.

And every time I think about how close I came to giving up—on this book, on this vision, on myself—I want to hug that version of me. There was a moment I almost scrapped this book title. There was a moment I considered walking away from the entire book. I didn't know how I'd fund it. Or find the time. Or pull from myself what needed to be created. But something in me—maybe that disco ball self—refused to quit.

Because if I had let someone else's opinion override my soul's truth, I would've let them talk me out of being me.

So consider this your rooftop rally cry: We don't need the watered-down version of you. We need the whole damn you. Your full expression. Your vibe. Your voice. Your vision. Not the filtered, people-pleasing edit. Not the safe and silent one. You are the original. You are the blueprint. You are the spark we've been waiting for. So the next time you scroll through your photos—whether from two years ago, two months ago, or even two days ago—I want you to feel proud. Proud of how far you've come. Proud of how you've hung in. Proud of the way you keep showing up. That evolution? That growth? That change? That's proof of life. And isn't that the whole point?

Here's to the beginning of all of our becomings.

She's a rebel,
climbing confidently up to her next level—
a constant source,
a powerful force.
She's the bass and the treble,
lit up like a turntable,
spinning hit after hit,
'cause she knows she is it.
And she doesn't quit
She never loses grip
of her dreams.
She's ready to be seen.
She's the whole symphony—
a maestro of manifestation,
a conductor of courage,
a melody of movement.
Note by note,
orchestrating her life
the way she wants.
Because she can,
so she does.
She's intentional,
non-conventional,
she's a rebel.

Fakers may take,
but they know they've got no grip on
my confidence—
'cause it's always bright
with the lights on.

NEVER

TRAPPED

ALWAYS

MAPPED

THE WAR OF ART

If you were to ask me which one book has changed my life the most—both personally and professionally—The War of Art by Steven Pressfield is easily in my top three. And just like I did with You Are a Badass by Jen Sincero, I've probably gifted this book to hundreds of people by now. I truly believe it's single-handedly responsible for the birth of so many blessings in my life.

Every single page is powerful, but my favorite is on page 142. Pressfield talks about fear—calling it resistance. He lists all the usual suspects: fear of being selfish, fear of poverty, fear of failure, fear of being ridiculous, fear of throwing it all away, fear of launching into the void, fear of madness, fear of death. And then he drops the real truth:

"While all of these are serious fears, they're not the real fear—the master fear—the mother of all fears that's so close to us that even when we verbalize it, we don't believe it. The fear that we will succeed. That we can access the powers we secretly know we possess. That we can become the person we sense in our hearts that we truly are."

I remember reading that and feeling shook to my core. I wasn't afraid of trying—I was afraid of thriving. I was scared of what would happen if it worked. Because if it did, what would change? Would I still be accepted? Would I know how to handle the abundance, the power, the visibility?

For me, the fear of success has always been the loudest one in the room. The fear of fully stepping into who I was born to be. But here's what I know now: that crown I was afraid to wear? It was mine all along.

If you've been playing it safe, holding back, doubting your power—this is your sign. You don't fear failing. You fear becoming. And that's exactly what you were born to do.

Mirror, mirror on the wall,
who is the fairest of them all?
I am.
I was.
And will always be.

REDEFINING SUCCESS

I once read a quote—and I wish I could find the exact words—but the message has never left me. I'll paraphrase: we spend our lives chasing everything—money, status, luxury, likes. But the moment our health is threatened, we only want one thing.

That one hit me hard. And it made me realize how distorted the word success has become. How deeply it bothers me. Somewhere along the way, success got reduced to a checklist: money, metrics, awards, first-class seats, and magazine spreads. We act like if we just hit those external milestones, we've "made it."

I even had a friend ask me at dinner once, "Would you say you've made it?" She's one of those big-question kind of gals—the kind who doesn't do small talk. I love that about her.

On paper, my answer was yes. I'm self-made. I built a seven-figure business. I wrote a bestselling book. I've shared stages with legends. I've been on magazine covers. I've won awards. I've built a brand.

On paper, yeah—it looks like I've made it.
But the real answer? Probably no.

Because I was still in a cage. Still afraid to fully self-express for fear of not getting booked, losing followers, or offending someone.

I was "successful." But I wasn't free.

I've since redefined success. These days, it looks like doing work you love, the way you want, with people who feel like soul fuel. It's not about performance—it's about alignment. It's not about proving—it's about being.

And that kind of success? It starts on the inside. Because no matter what you earn, build, or post—if you're not being you, it'll never feel like enough.

So here's a little nudge: Get clear on your own definition of success. Make sure it's yours—not one handed to you by culture, fear, or conditioning. Ask yourself: Does this version of success make me feel alive? Does it reflect who I really am? If not—rewrite it.

The truth is, success without self-expression is just performance in a prettier outfit. And you deserve more than that. You deserve to be free.

I don't bounce back, I levitate to the next level.

In a world that loves to fake it,
let's make it—
and keep on making it,
until the stars align
and history names it.

FLEXIBLITY

Let's talk about balance—the holy grail of modern life. Work-life balance. Hormonal balance. Inbox balance. We hear it all the time, like if we could just tweak the dials perfectly, we'd unlock some kind of secret level of peace. But here's the thing: true balance is a myth—at least if you're a human being living an actual, full-spectrum life.

Because life doesn't happen in perfectly measured increments. It happens in seasons. In surges. In tidal waves. And those waves? They're not asking for permission to crash. If you're launching something in your business, friendships and happy hours might take a backseat. If you're chasing toddlers around the house, self-care may get pushed to the edges. If you're navigating grief, love, transition, reinvention—something's going to fall out of frame. That's not failure. That's life.

As I write this, I'm in the thick of launching a book—writing, marketing, creating, planning. And let me tell you: a lot of things I love are not getting my energy right now. Not because they don't matter. But because there's only so much of me to go around.

So no—this isn't about balance. This is about flexibility.
And honestly? I like that better.

Because flexibility isn't just a cute productivity hack—it's a nervous system flex. The goal isn't to feel calm 24/7. That's not regulation—that's disassociation. True regulation is the ability to flow with life's inevitable chaos. To ride the wave without being swallowed. To move from grounded to activated and back again—with grace, not guilt.

Adaptability is the real magic. Especially in seasons of uncertainty. When we aim for balance, we chase perfection. But when we train for flexibility? We cultivate resilience. This is one of my favorite things about the improv theater. We're not seeking stillness—we're seeking responsiveness. We say yes. We let go. We meet the moment, not the plan. There is no script, no finish line—just a series of choices, made with presence.

So maybe the goal was never to be balanced.
Maybe the goal is to be bendy.

It's not about you against the world. It's about you attracting the world.

Sometimes I close my eyes and dream
of the future I'm destined to meet.
And in one of those midnight visions,
I found myself in transit—
walking big city streets,
chasing big city dreams.
Cool breeze. Neon haze.
Sidewalks humming with a thousand stories.
And there I was—just me—
until I turned a corner
and saw me
reflected on a stranger's tee.
My words.
Not on paper.
But screen-printed in bold across cotton.
Original verse.
A bar I'd once whispered to a page—
now moving through the world,
worn like armor,
etched with my becoming.
I froze.
Smiled.
Felt my breath catch like it knew.
Because though it took me a while,
I've come miles and miles
from who I used to be.
Finally free.
So me.
So I let it be.

I am grateful for this body—
the swerves and the curves,
the dimples and the dopeness,
the birthmarks and the bones,
every perfect imperfection
written in flesh and fire.

This body carries me.
This heart beats for me.
These lungs breathe for me.
Each breath a blessing
I didn't have to earn—
it just happens
without permission,
without performance.

I am a walking miracle.
A one-of-a-kind design.
Sacred by default.
Worthy by birthright.
Every scar is scripture.
Every curve, a psalm.
Every inch of me—
holy, whole, and home.

SEDUCTIVELY SLOW

There's something sacred about having the whole place to yourself. No one to talk to. No one to entertain. No one to perform for. Just me, the desert air, and a silence so wide it feels like a wink from the universe.

Listen, I love people. I love the mic. I live to shift the frequency inside convention centers and ballrooms. But after a keynote, I crash. I burn. I crave solitude like oxygen. After a recent sprint of travel, I needed a reset like my life depended on it. Because maybe it does. So I'm slowing down. And reimagining what "busy" means. Busy now looks like breathing. Like rest. Like nervous system repair—because mine? Is toast.

I've been grinding since I was thirteen. Conditioned for hustle.

Go. Go. Go.
Do. Do. Do.

But here's the kicker: according to my Human Design, I'm not built for that. I'm a 4/6 Projector. Translation? I don't generate my own energy. I'm not meant to force. I'm meant to see—and be seen. But I've been living like a generator on Red Bull, and my nervous system has been waving a white flag.

So now I'm working with a Human Design coach. And this week, she gave me the wildest assignment: move slower. Like... seductively slow. Silk-robe-on-a-staircase slow. Glass-of-wine, goddess-with-a-secret slow. Slow like I mean it. Slow like I'm in charge. Slow like I have nothing to prove.

And wow—does that feel weird. I've made a name for myself as the hype woman. The vibe dealer. The walking espresso shot. But now I'm starting to wonder—what if my real power isn't in the pace, but in the pause?

So here's the new energy: no more rushing. No more forcing. No more performing. Just presence. Just power. Just a regulated nervous system. Still vibes. Still hype. Just moving seductively slow.

Some say endings are final—
but she knows the truth:
they are doorways disguised as walls,
leading her through destiny's halls.
Completion. Closure. Endings.
But also—
beginnings.
Growth.
Change.
A sacred cycle.
A cosmic stage.
Reminding her to trust the rhythm of time,
to surrender sweetly,
to release,
to climb.
Like a snake, she sheds her skin.
Like a phoenix, she rises again.
As one chapter closes,
she collects her roses—
deeply knowing,
she's glowing,
illuminated in the fire of her own design,
moving boldly in the rhythm of 999.
Not just an ending,
but a sovereign sign—
completion is not where the story rests.
It's the spark
that ignites
what's coming next.

999

It came to me in a dream—999.

I had been deep in thought about when to release this book, knowing the timing had to feel just right. The spiritual girlie in me knew it needed to align with the moon, the stars, and maybe even a little numerology magic. So I started digging—flipping through calendars and dates—when September caught my eye. The ninth month. Hmmmm? Still trying to make sense of my 999 dream, I kept researching and stumbled onto a date that hit me like a lightning bolt: September 9, 2025.

9/9/2025. Add it up—2 + 0 + 2 + 5—and yep, that's a 9. Put all three together—999.

I felt the tears well up and put my hand on my heart, almost unable to breathe. I knew instantly: this was it. The divine sign I had been waiting for.

In numerology, 999 represents endings and new beginnings—a sacred cycle of completion and transformation. It honors the closing of one chapter while the next unfolds in divine timing. It felt like God was telling me it was time to move on—from grinding, hustling, proving, and processing pain—into an era of wisdom, beauty, abundance, and unapologetic creativity. A new chapter. A homecoming. A birth date. This book had to come out on 9/9/2025.

And the signs just keep coming.

In April 2025, I'll celebrate nine years as an entrepreneur.
I was born at 1:44—1 + 4 + 4 = 9.
The year 2025 itself is a universal 9 year. The year of the snake—symbol of transformation and shedding old skins.
In traditional BaZi Feng Shui, 2025's lucky number is 9—positioned in the east, exactly where my office sits in my house. And exactly where I wrote this book.

Everywhere I look, the nines keep showing up.
Winking at me.
Reminding me to trust what's next.

When you see 999, in this book, around my brand, and out in the wild—know it's a symbol of reinvention. Of laying down what no longer serves you. Of stepping boldly into new dimensions of yourself. 999 is more than a number. It's a mantra. It's a call to release what's done, and to welcome what's next. A reminder that nothing is wasted—Every ending is just the beginning of something wildly beautiful and new.

NEVER REJECTED
ALWAYS PROTECTED

ANGEL NUMBERS

A cosmic nudge. A wink from the Universe. A breadcrumb on your path. Let them guide you—and don't forget to holler back.

111 means new beginnings. Manifestation is in motion. Your thoughts are casting spells. Be intentional. Be bold. Be the vibe you want to attract.

222 is about balance and alignment. Trust the process. Your magic is marinating. Keep the faith. Stay soft and steady. It's working.

333 is divine support. Guidance from above. Your spirit team is loud and proud. You're surrounded. You're supported. Keep moving like you know they've got you.

444 brings foundation, protection, and stability. Trust. Know you are divinely protected and exactly where you're supposed to be. Ten toes down, baby.

555 signals big change, freedom, and transformation. The old you can't come with you. Buckle up. You're shape-shifting—and it's glorious.

666 is a call to realign, reflect, and refocus. Time to unplug and recalibrate. Drop the guilt. Pick up the mirror. What needs your attention?

777 is divine timing, inner wisdom, and a little cosmic luck. You're in sync with the Universe's playlist. Stay tuned in. This is your soulful jackpot.

888 is abundance, power, and infinite flow. The bag is on its way—but this isn't just about money. It's alignment, baby. You are the abundance.

999 marks completion, closure, and graduation. A cycle is ending—and a new one is being born. You're not just closing doors, you're stepping into portals. Celebrate what was. Prepare for what's next. You're being prepared for your next divine level.

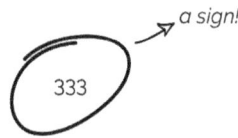

Liftoff.
Humans can do it too.
We don't need rockets to rise.
No jet fuel. No wings.
No runway beneath our feet.
We launch from within—
no plane in sight,
no command center calling the shots.
Because we are the command center.
Intuition: our navigator.
Belief: our fuel.
Vision: our sky.
We set direction daily,
charting new constellations
with nothing but courage,
desire,
and soul.
We rise—
as high as our dreams dare to reach,
as far as our desire will stretch,
as boundless as we're willing to trust
the fire inside us to catch.
No countdown.
No permission.
Just ignition.

LIKE AN ECLIPSE) ·) · ● · (· (I DON'T MISS

DREAMS VS GOALS

Dreams live deep in your soul. They are the big, beautiful what-ifs that keep you up at night. They go where you go—quietly whispering, patiently waiting for you to listen. Goals, on the other hand, are the action steps we take to bring those dreams to life.

If dreams are the vision, goals are the vehicle—the daily habits, intentional choices, and focused efforts that bridge the gap between where you are and where you want to be.

Consider the difference:
- Dream: Write my first novel.
- Goals: Cultivate a daily writing habit, explore publishing options, network with fellow authors, take a writing course, join a writing community.

Dreams are the destination.
Goals are the map.

Here's where it gets tricky: Most people get lost because they mistake one for the other. They either dream endlessly without taking action—or they set goals without a deeper dream to fuel them.

But here's the truth: Dreams require discipline. Goals require heart.

You can't just wish for something and expect it to happen. And you can't grind through a checklist that isn't rooted in what sets your soul on fire. And sometimes —when life shifts—the map has to change.

But the destination? That stays the same.

Maybe the route takes longer than expected.
Maybe you hit a detour.
Maybe you need to pause, pivot, or reimagine the path.

But if the dream is still calling to you... you keep going. Because dreams don't expire. They evolve. And the only way to reach them is to keep mapping your way forward—one brave goal at a time.

It's time to shake up the snow globe.
Drop a new beat.
Turn up the heat.
See, bread won't rise without yeast—
so hit the streets.
Wake up your inner beast.
Shake up what's been lying dormant inside,
and cast aside:
fear.
doubt.
comparison.
pride.
Ignite a fire from within.
Feel it deep in your bones,
in your soul,
in those sacred places only you know.
Because it's never too late—
not now,
not ever—
to begin again.

BE THE STORY

People always ask: How do I write an interesting book? How do I craft an original keynote? What stories should I tell? And my answer—always, forever—is this: go live an interesting life.

Do all the things. Make all the mistakes. Say yes to weird opportunities. Get your heart broken. Heal it. Fall down in public. Get up with style. Move cities. Change careers. Talk to strangers. Try the thing you're afraid of. Sit with the feelings you usually rush past. Dance in places you don't belong. Laugh in rooms that once scared you.

Because original work doesn't come from theory. It comes from living. It's earned—not curated. And the more honest your life, the more interesting your work. You don't find your material. You live it. And then you tell us all about it.

That's how we re-create ourselves. That's how we write things worth reading. That's how we leave a mark.

Be the story. Then tell it like only you can.

I'm leaping into this dream—
this feeling I feel,
this world I can see,
and the visions that won't let me be—
that stir me in my sleep,
showing me a world of possibility
that sparkles like Tiffany.
As I orchestrate this symphony,
moving through the world differently—
no longer timidly,
not waiting for validity—
finding my way instantly
back home
to my brilliancy.

IF YOU WANT TO GO SOMEWHERE NEW THEN YOU HAVE TO LEAVE WHERE YOU ARE

She rides the waves—
her high of highs,
her low of lows.
And
    Y O
when she's good, she's gooooood.
But when she's bad?
She's baaaaad.
One wave keeps her stuck in the past.
The other puts her confidence on blast,
making her feel gifted, lifted,
charged with ascension—
as she shifts into another dimension.
Cosmically pulled.
A knowing deep down in her bones.
A whole new world,
yet a place she already knows.
Like she's been there before—
a déjà vu of sorts.
She can't help but want more.
So if that's what it takes
to feel divine reinvention—
she'll ride the waves,
make her mistakes,
clap back at the hate,
speak truth,
liberate,
and create.
As she makes her way down
the yellow brick road,
grabbing her crown,
assuming her position on the throne—
knowing there's no place like home:
that place in her soul
nobody else knows.

SELF-EXPRESSION ISN'T SOFT

In the future of work, self-expression won't be a soft skill—it'll be a survival skill. Because the leaders, teams, and cultures that thrive won't just be the ones who perform under pressure—they'll be the ones who know who they are under pressure, and act from that place with clarity, courage, and alignment anyway.

That's what Self-Expressionism is all about. It's not ego. It's not fluff. It's not a talent reserved for artists or extroverts. It's a soul-driven leadership philosophy designed for this new world of work. It's about congruence over performance. Alignment over image. Depth over dazzle. It's how we build cultures of trust, innovation, and resilience from the inside out.

This isn't just about well-being—it's about awareness. It's about knowing who you are so you can lead yourself, before leading others. Because when people lead from identity—not insecurity—they make braver choices. They build better relationships. They move faster with less burnout and more momentum. The future doesn't belong to those who hustle harder. It belongs to those who express more honestly. Because people don't burn out from doing too much—they burn out from pretending too long.

The old playbook is crumbling. The masks are cracking. What's needed now? Humanity. Awareness. Individuality. People who can think for themselves. People who trust themselves. People who can express new ideas without fear, and speak up without shapeshifting. In a world driven by AI, automation, and algorithmic perfection—soul will be the ultimate differentiator.

So if you've ever been told you're "too much," or felt the pressure to water yourself down, don't. You're not here to be digestible. You're here to be undeniable. And the more you honor that voice inside you—the louder your impact becomes.

Because being yourself isn't just spiritual. It's strategic. It's how we future-proof leadership. It's how we unlock creative performance. And it's how we build a future that works for all of us—not just the loudest or the safest, but the realest.

VIBRATION OF SUCCESS

Success has a vibration—a frequency that hums with the sweetness of joy, independence, security, comfort, sophistication, and prosperity. It's not just about wealth or status, but about the feeling of being deeply rooted in your own personal power. This internal queendom that only you possess—the sheer audacity of your presence.

When you tap into this vibration, any chip on your shoulder dissolves, bitterness melts away, and you'll never be a victim in this life. Why? Because you've realized that your internal light is the one true way to the infinite safety and success you crave.

It's time to step into the garden of your greatness because you've done the work, now you can trust that your harvest will arrive. You don't have to fake it or force it because you ARE IT.

So, this is your moment to dance and rejoice in the success you've earned. You know who you are. You know your true essence. You're not imitating anyone else—you're expressing your own vibe, radiating your blessings, and the world responds in kind. This is how success works when you're walking in the world as nothing but yourself—confident, vibrant, and unapologetically aligned.

Find contentment in this mission and radiate it on purpose.

Let your vitality, presence, and love be the loudest thing in any room you walk into. Trust that walking as your whole self creates a funnel for material magic and success. The vibration of success isn't something you chase—it's something you become. And you have become it—so it's time to be it.

She feels it—
a sweet stirring in her soul,
deep down in her bones,
where old whispers echo
and something ancient groans.
It's time to let go
of doing what she's told—
the shape that was borrowed,
the stories she outgrew,
the silence she sold.
No longer controlled,
she shatters the mold
as her new life unfolds—
not rushed, but revealed,
like gold pulled from stone.
Her essence, now exposed,
calls her home—
not back,
but forward,
to a throne carved in her own name.
A return.
A rise.
A flame.
A sight to behold.

EMOTIONAL SCALE

The Emotional Guidance Scale—a powerful tool inspired by Abraham Hicks—has helped me self-express, protect my energy, and feel good faster, even when things aren't good. Life throws curveballs: bad days, big bills, setbacks, and spilled coffee on your hot pink suit ten minutes before showtime. But here's what I've learned: feeling good is the goal—and it's the fastest way to get where you want to go.

It's not about denying your feelings—it's about guiding them so you don't get stuck. If you're feeling depressed (the lowest point on the scale), guess what? Anger is progress. Blame is progress. Worry is progress. Why? Because they're higher on the scale. They're a step up.

Too often, people judge progress without knowing the starting point. Someone might criticize your anger, but they don't know you've been stuck in despair—and anger, while uncomfortable, is your way out. Their feedback? Irrelevant.

Here's what blew my mind: jealousy is lower on the scale than hatred, rage, and anger. When you sit in jealousy and comparison, you vibrate at one of the lowest frequencies possible—trapped in lack, insecurity, and feeling less than. No wonder jealousy keeps you broke, stuck, and miserable.

But the moment you recognize that feeling, you can reach for a better one. Instead of dreading a dentist appointment, say: "I'm grateful I have healthy teeth and a doctor who takes care of me." Instead of groaning about taxes, try: "I'm proud I have income, a job, and money to manage." When cleaning the house, love bomb the space: "I love this home. I love my couch, my bed, my windows, my clothes. I love the comfort it provides me."

Same situations. Different energy.

Staying stuck in low vibrations—anger, guilt, jealousy—will keep you trapped longer than necessary. It doesn't mean you deny those feelings. It means you lead yourself through them. Every setback is happening for you, not to you. Feelings are temporary. You get to choose how long you stay there.

#	Abraham Hicks Emotional Guidance Scale	
1	Joy / Appreciation / Empowered / Freedom / Love	High Vibration
2	Passion	
3	Enthusiasm / Eagerness / Happiness	
4	Positive Expectation / Belief	
5	Optimism	
6	Hopefulness	
7	Satisfaction / Contentment	
8	Boredom	
9	Pessimism	
10	Frustration / Irritation / Impatience	
11	Overwhelmed	
12	Disappointment	
13	Doubt	
14	Worry	
15	Blame	
16	Discouragement	
17	Anger	Low Vibration
18	Revenge	
19	Hatred / Rage	
20	Jealousy	
21	Insecurity / Guilt / Unworthiness	
22	Fear / Grief / Depression / Despair / Powerlessness	

I keep the Emotional Guidance Scale taped to my computer as a daily reminder to reach for the better-feeling thought, no matter what's happening. Because here's the truth: Feeling good is not selfish. It's strategic. Your vibration is everything.

Protect it at all costs.

You were born with all the stars in the sky—
don't forget to look inside.

RADICAL ORIGINALITY

Radical originality isn't about being loud. It's not about saying the wildest thing in the room. It's not about hot pink or graffiti jackets (even though you know I live for both). It's not even about being liked.

It's about being real.

Originality is a deep internal knowing that becomes an external force—and that force becomes unmistakable the moment you walk into a room.

We've been conditioned to think originality looks like flash, like branding, like noise. But I want to offer something different: originality is your engine.

You might not see it at first glance, but it's there. Think of a Ferrari. No one sees the engine when it flies by. They see the exterior, the badge, the vibe. But the Ferrari knows—it's built with something rare under the hood. That's what makes it powerful. Not the paint job. Not the logo. The engine.

You have that too.

So the question becomes: what's your engine made of? What were you born with that no one can copy? What do you believe in so deeply that it fuels every move you make? What are you here to say, to stand for, to shift?

Because when you know your engine—when you know who you are—you stop outsourcing your originality. You stop performing for approval. You stop shape-shifting to fit in. You start driving in your own lane, in your own way, at your own speed.

And sure, not everyone will get it. I can name a handful of people who are radically original—and totally not my vibe. But I still respect it. Because I know what it takes to say, "This is me."

Radical originality is really just radical courage. The courage to show up. To stand out. To be you. To say, "I'm not here to make you like me—I'm here because I like me."

The realest ones in the room? They're not always the loudest.
They're the truest

I'm rich with talent,
catching dreams with talons,
taking flight in full balance,
fully claiming my palace.
And just like Alice
in Wonderland—
I wonder, man...
what if wonder can
be the master plan?

STEP INTO THE LIGHT

It's time to come out of the cave and step into the light because your truth and the full expression of you is what the world needs now more than ever. If you are reading this right now you are being called to share your voice and fully self-express. And there has never been a better time in history to do just that. To rise up, be yourself, and let your soul's voice echo into the world.

Whether it's through writing, speaking, singing, or any other form of creative expression, your soul is yours alone—shaped through lifetimes of growth, hardship, wisdom, and experience. When shared, it becomes your truth, making you uniquely and powerfully you.

Deep down in your soul lies a voice that's been sculpted by legacy, history, and evolution. It's not just a sound. It's a frequency. Your individual voice is the most powerful sound on the planet—its vibration is seismic, and it can't be silenced. Every time you express yourself and reveal the truth that only you know, you don't just heal yourself—you heal everyone who receives your message.

It's time to strip away the layers of conditioning that have kept you small, safe, and afraid. Let your unique soul sing, speak, create, and unapologetically be. Because when you do, you discover that you actually have a clear mission and a powerful message. And the more you share it, the clearer it becomes.

If you feel afraid of this, know you're not alone. It's normal to fear judgment or worry that your voice doesn't matter. But here's the truth: What the world needs now more than ever is not cave women but lightworkers and earth angels who aren't afraid to fly—high up into the sky, linking arms with the women in their tribe, helping them soar even higher.

So come out of the cave.
Step into the light.
Because what the world needs right now is you.

A new art form is being born—
where courage wears the crown,
and self-expression reigns supreme.
Life itself: the bold blank canvas.
And the masterpiece?
Your very existence.
A bespoke collection of:
color.
magic.
soul.
energy.
A cosmically curated palette,
streaked with brushstrokes of brilliance—
thanks to your resilience,
your realness,
your refusal to hide.
Because the composition of you
is unapologetically original—
a wild, wonder-filled manifesto:
more Basquiat than beige,
more scream than silence,
more heart than hollow.
A gallery of:
courage.
wisdom.
fire.
and heart.
You are not just the artist.
You are the art.

THE BOX

Don't waste another dime—or another second—trying to squeeze yourself into a box that was never big enough for you anyway.

Make moves.
Self-express.
Wake up 8-year-old you.
Hone your focus.
Listen to your intuition.
Wear what you want.
Tighten your circle.
Simplify your life.
Travel.
Take risks.
Try new sh*t.
Get uncomfortable daily.
Call your shot.
Unplug from the matrix.
Sweat.
Read.
Regulate your nervous system.
Get outside.
Unplug from the matrix.
Breathe deeply.
Trust yourself.
Holler.

She reaches for the stars—
then multiplies them with her touch.
They may think she's too much,
but she knows she's enough.
A mirror of her creator,
a divine co-illustrator,
aligned with something greater.

RECREATE

Ever notice how the word recreation holds re-create right inside it? That's no accident. It's a divine wink. Because in order to re-create anything—yourself, your energy, your business, your brand, your body, your relationship, your vibe—it's going to require recreation.

Recreation is required for reinvention.

It's not just a vacation. It's not just a hobby. It's an intentional pause—a deliberate detour from the matrix—so you can reconnect with your soul. It's the act of getting out into the world to remember what it means to feel fully alive. To experience joy for joy's sake. To stop performing and start being.

People ask me all the time how to write an good book, give a killer keynote, or live a more creative life. My answer? Go live a more interesting life. Unplug. Take a walk. Hike a trail. Jump in a pool. Book the trip. Try the thing. Sit with yourself under the damn moon. Recreation fuels imagination, and imagination is the portal to your next evolution.

So if you're stuck, overwhelmed, uninspired—or just feeling a little too online—consider this your sign to go play. To go wander. To go re-create.

You don't need another to-do list.
You may just need a little more joy.

THE MUSE IN THE ROOM

Sometimes your next idea isn't in the strategy. It's in the room.

For me? It's a 1980 Street Rocker boombox that sits in the center of my office. Big, bold, and unapologetically analog. It doesn't blend in—it booms. And that's exactly the point.

That boombox is more than a nostalgic artifact. It's a reminder of who I am, where I came from, and what I'm here to do. It keeps me rooted in rhythm, culture, curiosity, and creativity. It reminds me to turn up the volume on what matters. To be bold. To stay analog in a digital world. To honor the mixtape era I was raised in—when originality reigned and voices were raw. It's not just décor. It's part of my creative DNA.

And while the boombox is my current muse, it took a whole parade of muses to get me here: flamingos, disco balls, crowns, cheetahs, mixtapes, palm trees, lightning bolts. I've loved them all. I've anchored into each of them. Every one helped unlock a new piece of my voice—a breadcrumb leading me home.

Right now, it's the boombox. And I have a feeling she'll be with me for a while. But I also hope she evolves. Because I will. And that's the point. This isn't about collecting things. It's about staying awake. Your muse doesn't have to make sense to anyone else. What matters is that you have one. That you're actively participating in the life you're living. That you're tuned in, turned on, and tapped into the beauty that moves your soul forward.

So look around. Your home. Your workspace. Your memories.

What object keeps showing up in your orbit?
What symbol, shape, or icon lights you up?
What did you collect, doodle, or obsess over as a kid?
What's the one thing that just feels like you?

Pick one. Place it somewhere sacred. Let it guide your next creation, your next idea, your next evolution. Because sometimes, the most powerful way to move forward… is to remember where the beat began. So dust off your dreams. Turn up the truth. And press play.

What does she have to lose—
when she has nothing to prove?
The opposite of dependence—
a divine superintendence.
A bold amendment
to the original intention:
following someone else's agenda.
All that bending and
extending and
defending and
pretending—
left her full of resentment.
So she took the cement
and turned it into a pendant,
wrapped it around her neck like a lesson.
And like a lieutenant,
she salutes her independence—
not as rebellion,
but as resurrection.

SUMMON YOUR CREATIVITY

— Revisit your childhood bedroom. What's still true? What got lost?
— Go thrift shopping. Build a look from one unexpected item.
— Book a photo shoot. Hire a stylist. Create a persona.
— Take yourself to a museum and write a poem about one piece.
— Watch live music. Feel it in your bones.
— Plan a Ferris Bueller-style day off. No guilt. All play.
— Buy a blank notebook and design your own cover. Make it your idea vault.
— Host a "weird ideas only" dinner party. No small talk allowed.
— Visit a plant shop. Pick the one that calls to you. Name it.
— Learn a new skill with your hands: pottery, knitting, woodworking.
— Read biographies of wild, original people.
— Court your creativity—take it on actual dates.
— Pull oracle or tarot cards and journal whatever comes up.
— Visit a record store. Pick something based on the cover alone.
— Write a love letter to your future self.
— Try spoken word poetry—read it to yourself in the mirror.
— Make a mood board for your next era. Go big. Go wild.
— Create a personal altar or vibe corner in your home. Let it evolve with you.
— Ask your 8-year-old self what they'd do today—and do it.
— Write a manifesto and post it on your fridge. Rewrite as needed.
— Interview your grandparents, parents, or chosen family about their younger selves.
— Visit an art supply store. Buy something you don't know how to use.
— Start your own holiday. Celebrate it however you want.
— Write to Hans Zimmer and let his soundtracks score your next idea.
— Watch stand-up comedy. Laugh 'til your stomach hurts.
— Walk through a luxury mall playing jazz in your AirPods. Study the windows.
— Study your Human Design chart. (You're encoded with brilliance.)
— Sleep with a notebook next to your bed. Dreams hold downloads.
— Go to a park. Lay in the grass. Bring a notebook and some rosé.
— Book a solo trip. Explore somewhere you've never been.
— Pick one day a week to self-express on social media and share your art.
(Join the movement at #SelfExpressionSunday on Instagram.)

I am not here to be a caretaker
for those who ghost their inner chambers.
If you aren't sitting with your shadows,
if you don't have an open mind,
if you haven't cleaned up the hallways
of your house—
then I will kindly,
respectfully,
courageously,
and immediately
be stepping out of your aura
to protect mine.

LEGACY

As I approach 50 (a number that still feels surreal to say out loud), I think about legacy a lot. It used to feel like one of those big, shiny words we toss around—something reserved for wills, eulogies, or statues built long after we're gone.

But the shift that changed everything? Legacy isn't what you leave behind. It's what you do right now. It's the risks you take. The art you make. The truth you speak. The people you pour into. The energy you carry into the room—and the ripple you leave behind.

And what's wild is how many people have left that kind of mark on me without even realizing it.

Like the Jazzercise instructor in the '90s who preached eye cream to us teen girls. I still think of her every morning when I tap it on. Or the girl in my sorority who taught me to apply mascara—both sides of the lash. I still do it her way. Or Mrs. Brown, my fifth-grade teacher, who signed me up for my first speech meet and changed my life forever. Or my Aunt Dino—bold, brilliant, childfree, and rule-breaking. She didn't ask permission. She made her own path. And in doing so, she lit mine.

None of them were trying to be remembered. They were just living their truth. That's legacy.

Even as a professional speaker, I'm not on stage hoping everyone likes me. That's a trap. I create what lights me up. What I wish I had heard. What's helped me find my way. That kind of realness? People feel it.

So I always say: don't create for the audience—create from your soul. If it's real to you, it will resonate. And when it resonates, it lives on.

Now, before every keynote, I don't pray to be liked. I pray for courage. To say the thing that needs to be said—for the one person who needs it most.

Because legacy isn't built in monuments.
It's built in moments.

ink of a self-expressionist
(a mantra for the bold & becoming)

I vow to show up unedited—
to walk into rooms with all of me,
proudly hollering at my dreams,
trusting my timing, honoring my rhythm,
and creating from the fire in my soul.

I release the need for perfection.
I choose presence over performance.
I trade applause for alignment.
I let my truth be louder than their doubt.

When fear visits, I don't shrink—I stand tall.
When resistance rises, I don't quit—I create.
When comfort tempts me, I don't settle—I evolve.

I'm not here to fit in.
I'm here to pop off.

This is my era of living fully expressed—
of infinite potential.

I will not delay.
I will not betray myself to belong.

I create from love.
I move with intention.
I lead with soul.

I am the art.
I am the brush.
I am the bold color
on the canvas of my life.

And I'm just getting started.

INTENTION ENERGIZES

ATTENTION TRANSFORMS

5D Dopeness

On a steamy September day in Phoenix, Arizona, I went into the city to attend my first-ever Abraham Hicks event.

For those unfamiliar: Abraham Hicks is the name given to a collective consciousness channeled by author and speaker Esther Hicks. Their teachings are rooted in the law of attraction, vibrational alignment, and the power of thought as a creative force. Some call it spiritual. Some call it quantum. Me? I call it 5D dopeness.

And while I left that day with a notebook full of notes and holy wow moments, I distilled it down to my Top 10 takeaways—ones I keep pinned on my wall to this day. They realign me when I spiral. They ground me when I fly too high. They remind me who I am and what I came here to do.

Abraham Hicks Event
September 21, 2024 | Phoenix, AZ | Hyatt Regency

1. Get to feeling good—fast. You can't attract what you do want if you're focused on what you don't want. Ask yourself: are your words stronger for what you don't have than what you desire?
2. Tension is a sign you've deviated from who you really are.
3. My way of living doesn't have to be yours.
4. Never make decisions from a place of urgency.
5. Don't sell yourself. Be yourself.
6. You'll always take you with you.
7. Start where you are. Then go where you want.
8. The universe responds to thought.
9. Your life is a mirror of your emotional trends.
10. I came. I'm good. I'm figuring it out.

May they do for you what they continue to do for me: bring you back to your knowing, back to your alignment, and back to your own brand of 5D dopeness.

She is made up of stardust and spit—
a cocktail of cosmos that just won't quit.
One part magic. One part fire.
Infinite potential. Relentless desire.

She walked the galaxies with her gaze,
pride in her stride,
and under the moonlight of her own becoming,
she hollered her dreams into the sky.

Audacity in her aura.
Truth in her bones.
She doesn't wait to get beamed up—
she builds her own rocket ship
and calls in Source to help fly her home.

She's not afraid to fall apart.
She's not afraid to shine.
She's glitter and grit,
rebellion and rhythm,
elegance by design.

She's softness with structure.
She's steel-laced with soul.
This is what it looks like
to both surrender and control.

She's made of stardust and spit—
wildly woven. Divinely lit.
Not here to fit in or stand still—
she's here to shift dimensions
and bend the light in new directions.

NO GOING BACK

We aren't going back, baby.

We're moving forward—

into unlimited possibility,
into divine stability,
into higher vibrations,
into new dimensions,
into dope conversations,
into electric energy,
into unapologetic boundaries,
into the realest realness,
into ultimate uniqueness,
into moving with the moon,
into Aquarius,
into abundance,
into the best version of ourselves,
into crowning ourselves queens,
into HOLLERING at our dreams.

What's your favorite color?

Rainbow.

Why?

Because I have a bright future.

— Kiley

Footnote:
This rainbow-inspired gem came straight from the heart of my niece, Kiley Grace, during a lunch date in The Lou (St. Louis) in May 2025. I asked her what her favorite color was, and without missing a beat, she said "rainbow—duh, because I have a bright future!" That moment lit me up. Sometimes the clearest wisdom comes from the smallest voices. This piece is a reminder that confidence, optimism, and color don't have to fade as we grow older—unless we let them.

HOW TO BE THE ART

Living like a self-expressionist doesn't require fancy degrees or flawless confidence. It doesn't mean being loud, perfect, or even sure of yourself. It simply requires one thing: presence. The kind that listens deeply. Creates consistently. Speaks truth out loud—even when your voice shakes. To live a self-expressed life is to become the art—not just admire it from afar.

So how do you summon that inner artist? Here's what I've learned:

1. Declare yourself the art.
I'll never forget the summer I said those four words out loud: "I am an artist." To someone else. Out loud. In public. No explanation. No disclaimers. Just truth. And something shifted immediately because words are wands. You can cast spells with your words—on your life, your future, your identity. So speak it, claim it, own it, be it. Anoint thyself.

2. Make self-expression a sacred ritual.
Whether it's a daily voice memo to your future self, freewriting over coffee, dance breaks in your kitchen, or doodles in your dream journal, carve out time to listen to your soul. Ten sacred minutes is enough. What matters is that you're consistent—and intentional.

3. Be it before you see it.
We're done faking it till we make it. Now we make it till we become it. Self-expression is about stepping into the version of yourself that already exists—before the world gives you permission. Be the poet, the speaker, the entrepreneur, the healer, the creative badass before the stage, the book deal, or the applause arrives.

4. Build your creative altar.
I keep a 1980s street rocker boombox in my office. Crystals. Disco balls. The goddess Lakshmi. Candles. Card decks. Things that remind me of who I am and where I'm going. What could that be for you? A vinyl collection? A wall of affirmations? A Polaroid camera? Build a vibe that brings you back home to yourself.

5. Live an interesting life.
You want to write interesting stories? Tell magnetic truths? Build something original? Go live. Talk to strangers. Go on solo trips. Take classes. Make mistakes. Follow the spark. The most original content always comes from living—not just scrolling.

6. Create on the edges.
Your power lives in the borderlands—between comfort and discomfort, knowing and not knowing. So go to your edge. Say the thing that scares you. Wear what feels like you. Share the art that's still raw. The edge is where the gold lives.

7. Protect your weird.
Your quirks, your contradictions, your essence—this is your soul logo. The moment you start diluting it to be more palatable or productive or popular, you start losing your signal. Guard your originality like your life depends on it. Because it kinda does.

I want you to know:
You sit on a throne.
Walking a path only you can own.
Directly in line with where you're meant to go.
Standing in truth,
growing roots before fruit —
trusting the pace, the palette,
and the knowing that the path ahead is divinely designed.
You are a canvas kissed by sacred time.
Each brushstroke: presence.
Each breath: a present.
You, beloved, are the gift.
To this world.
To your world.
To everyone who steps into your aura.
You are appointed.
You are anointed.
Here on a mission,
with sacred ambition —
complete soul ignition.
So, as you shift into new dimensions,
and your legacy levitates into cosmic ascensions,
you'll be tried,
you'll be tested,
you'll even second-guess it.
But when that happens,
pick up the phone
and call your one precious, wildly dope soul back home —
because you were never lost.
Only being shown.

"NO FORCE ON EARTH CAN STOP WHAT'S DIVINELY YOURS"

THE NEXT LEVEL

Don't be in such a rush to upgrade your life that you forget how good your life already is. Your future's on its way—no matter what. But gratitude? Gratitude is how you meet it with power. It's the real flex.

Because if you can't get down with the blessings you've already got, what makes you think you're ready for more? The way you treat your current level is the audition for your next one. Want more? Start by honoring what's already in front of you. Be wildly thankful for the home you live in now. The breath in your lungs. Every dollar in your account. The wisdom in your bones. Say thank you—out loud. Often.

And let's be real: if you can't even accept a compliment, how are you gonna accept a million-dollar check one day? Someone says, "You look amazing," and you reply, "Oh gosh, no—I'm a mess"? That's not humility. That's resistance. And honestly? It short-circuits the moment. You know how it feels when you give someone a genuine compliment and they brush it off? Weird, right?

Let's stop doing that.

From here on out, we receive compliments. Fully. We say, "Thank you." We let it land. We let it feel good. Because that's what the next level demands of us: the ability to receive.

Same goes for support. Like when I'm on a plane and someone offers to lift my carry-on into the overhead bin. I used to swat that help away. Now? I smile and say, "Yes, thank you so much." I let people help. I let people give. I let it be easy.

Because receiving isn't weakness—it's wisdom. And if you're serious about rising higher, the real question isn't "How hard are you willing to work?" It's "How open are you willing to be?"

So start where you are. Celebrate what's already working. Tend to it. Appreciate it. Because the next level doesn't always knock. Sometimes, it waits—for the moment you're ready to receive it.

I call forth all my angels—
my cosmic helpers in the subtle realms—
to be with me.
Here.
Now.
Always,
As I summon new ways
to live my days
unapologetically—
more free.
More me.
I ask for divine orchestration
to bless this ceremonial occasion.
No need for force
or false persuasion,
as I rise into higher vibration.
As I move through sacred activation,
only calling in what's mine,
by divine decree,
hollering at dreams
that finally feel like me.

POP ART

I've always been drawn to the kind of art that doesn't whisper—it shouts. The kind that punches you in the chest with color, courage, and a deep "I-don't-give-a-damn-if-you-get-it" energy. Expressionism. Pop art. Graffiti. Street art. That beautiful rebellion on canvas.

Expressionism started as a protest. Artists like Edvard Munch and Egon Schiele distorted reality to show you what life felt like—not what it looked like. Emotion over perfection. Truth over technique. That rawness? That was the point.

Fast forward to Basquiat—one of the baddest to ever do it. He exploded onto the scene with bold lines, raw poetry, and frenetic energy that refused to be tamed. His work screamed of race, power, identity, and pain. He painted like he was on fire. And honestly? He was.

Picasso, the rebel of form, ripped up the rulebook and rewrote it in angles. He said, "Learn the rules like a pro, so you can break them like an artist." (My kind of guy.)

Add in Keith Haring's bold lines and activist heart. Banksy's cheeky truth bombs. Nina Chanel Abney's technicolor social commentary. These artists don't just paint—they holler.

Let their work remind you: You are a canvas. Your color is welcome here. Your edges, your truth—that is your art. Paint outside the lines. Be abstract. Be bright. Be loud. Be free.

You don't have to make sense to be brilliant.
You just have to show up with soul.

Spirit—
can you hear her?
She's soft.
She's sweet.
She's subtle.
But she's there.
Her essence.
And it carries a message —
effervescent.
A blessing.
She doesn't shout.
She doesn't rush.
She waits.
And when Spirit finally leans in,
she hears her whispers.
She was never lost.
She'd just been listening
to the wrong voice,
so she rose up
and made a new choice:
Herself—
and heard her soul rejoice.

1211

Do you have a number?

Maybe it's an angel number. Maybe it's just a sequence that follows you like a shadow. But some numbers? They're not random. They're revelations. Winks from the universe that whisper: keep going—you're right on time.

Mine is 1211.

It's lived in my bones for as long as I can remember—so much so, I tattooed it on my body. For years, it was my PIN, my password, my anchor. I didn't question it. I just knew. And as life unfolded, the meaning revealed itself in wild and wondrous ways.

I met my husband in December 2011. His birthday? 12/11. His boys' soccer numbers? 12 and 11. The cab number that picked us up the weekend we got engaged? 1211. My best friend? Born at 12:11. Our honeymoon hotel room? 1211. My very first keynote flight? Landed at 12:11. Even Uncle Jimmy—artist, drummer, soul on fire—left this earth on December 11.

And the list goes on: voice memos, receipts, timestamps, seat assignments. That number keeps showing up. Not because I'm lucky—but because I'm looking. Because I'm awake. Because I believe.

In numerology, 1 + 2 + 1 + 1 = 5. The number of the freedom-seeker. The wild child. The expressionist. That's not coincidence. That's confirmation. That's me—in numbers.

And here's what I've learned: having something like this—a number, a sign, a sacred code—shifts how you move through the world. You stop scanning for bad news and start watching for wonder. You feel supported. You trust the timing. You stay in rhythm with what's real.

So ask yourself: what's been trying to get your attention lately? What numbers show up when you're lost—or on the edge of something big? What keeps repeating in ways you can't explain? Because once you find your number, it's no longer just a number. It's a message. A mantra. A frequency. A flashlight. A reminder that your dreams aren't random—they're assigned.

She saw it first—with her eyes closed.
A universe only her soul could decode.
Stars bent for her belief.
Confidence giving her relief.
Fear fleeing like a thief.
She hollered at her dreams—
and they answered.
Parting seas,
immediately,
shifting her frequency.
New timeline.
New code.
New crown.
New dimension.
She didn't manifest it.
She expressed it.

THE PARADOX OF RULES

Rules aren't cages—they're containers. And freedom without structure? That's chaos. Confusion. Burnout. Overwhelm. A Pinterest board full of inspiration with no action.

True freedom is being able to choose your structure. And the most self-expressed people I know? They don't follow everyone else's rules. They write their own.

Because here's the truth: every rebel has rules. Every icon. Every artist. Every visionary. They may not look like "rules," but they have standards. Frameworks. Boundaries. Values. Soul laws. And those self-created rules? They're sacred.

They're not there to restrict you. They're there to protect you. They keep your energy focused. They keep your nervous system calm. They're bumpers on your bowling lane so you can roll heavy and still hit your target.

So no, these aren't the rules you've been handed. They're the rules you remember. The ones that make you more you. The ones you break—when breaking them means becoming someone braver.

This is the paradox we hold in Self-Expressionism: we honor rules not to be ruled, but to rule ourselves. Because when you know who you are—you lead yourself. And that's where peace lives.

All hail the Queen.

In moments before the sweet surrender of slumber,
as she drifts into theta,
she plants subliminal seeds—
shaping who she wants to be.
Seeing her legacy.
Feeling her frequency.
Knowing her destiny.
Waking up deciding that,
instead of waiting to meet her one day—
she'd become her today.
As if it's already hers.
As if she already is.
Already her.

THETA WAVES

Did you know that when you sleep, your body isn't just resting—it's rebuilding? Seriously. Your cells are regenerating, your mind is processing the day, and your subconscious is wide open. It's one of the most intuitive, magnetic windows of your entire day.

There's actual science behind it: during sleep, your brain consolidates memories, regulates emotions, and detoxes from stress. But here's where it gets wild—as you drift into sleep, your brain produces theta waves, the same slow-frequency brainwaves associated with deep meditation, creativity, intuition, and the subconscious mind. This is your brain's most receptive, imaginative state—the ideal zone for clarity, insight, and spiritual downloads.

So I started a ritual: every night before bed, I ask God, Source, the universe—for guidance. I'll literally toss a question into the dark, no pressure. Sometimes the answer shows up in a dream. Sometimes I wake up with an unexpected idea or peaceful knowing. It's like the universe slid into my subconscious DMs.

But here's the thing—what you do before sleep matters. A lot.

If you're falling asleep to chaos—true crime, anxiety scrolling, drama loops—your subconscious is marinating in that energy. That's the playlist your soul is absorbing on repeat. The last thing you take into sleep tends to manifest. So protect that portal.

Read a few pages of something nourishing. Journal a gratitude list. Write down a question you want answered. Listen to a theta-wave meditation on YouTube. I keep a notebook by my bed because some of my best ideas have arrived at 3:00 a.m. Like homework from the universe.

If you struggle with anxiety, depression, or panic (hand raised here), treat bedtime like a sacred manifesting ritual. Ask. Listen. Let your subconscious go to work. You might just wake up with a little more peace, a little more clarity—and a whole lot of magic.

Sweet dreams.
Happy manifesting.
Theta wave, activated.

Outdated ways of thinking.
Old rules for being.
Cages for creativity.
Boxes for boldness.
Closed doors on possibility.
Tears from trolling.
Hearts breaking over misunderstanding—
the pain of being seen but not got.
Silencing the spark
in every artist's heart.
But a new day is coming.
A new dawn is rising.
Where soul is syllabus.
Intuition is instructor.
Faith is louder than fear.
And truth stands taller than doubt.
Where we don't ask for permission—
we remember who we are.
Where "too much" is a compliment.
Where softness is strength,
and presence is power.
This isn't curriculum.
It's a calling.
This isn't memorization.
It's remembering.
Out with the old school,
in with Soul School.

GAINS

If hustle had a math equation, it'd be this:

Hard work + Consistency × Time = Results

I learned this from my trainer—shout out Brian White—who says a version of this on repeat. And honestly? It's not just the secret to getting gains in the gym—it's the secret to getting stronger in life.

When I show up to train, I'm not just chasing aesthetic goals or bikini-bod vibes. I'm working out for 90-year-old Judi. Every rep I do ensures she ages with as much ease as possible (because it's coming, like it or not), and is one less day—God willing—that I spend in a nursing home.

This philosophy—hard work, done consistently, over time—has changed the way I think. About results. About health. About business. About relationships.

We live in a world that sells us quick fixes and five-second fame. A culture obsessed with speed and virality.

Once upon a time, you had seven seconds to catch someone's attention. Now? Try two. That's the average attention span on social media in 2025. No wonder we're all frazzled.

But here's what never goes out of style: showing up. Day after day. Rep after rep.

Because effort, consistency, and time are the true holy trinity.

365 DAYS 365 WAYS

A queen thinks by design—
not by default.
Her thoughts serve her throne.
Never walking alone.
Her life, a collaboration
with the stars—
always mapping
what she can't see yet,
but knows will happen.
As she turns her realm into satin,
she summons her dragons
to burn doubt like a pattern.
Still stool, but unfastened,
she softens her edges—
gliding back home
to her sacred garden,
where roots beg her pardon.
Soft like cotton.
Most uncommon.
Never forgotten.
Forever sovereign.

PERSONAL REALITY

Joe Dispenza said it best: "Your personality creates your personal reality." And yo, that's the whole sermon. Because if you move like a victim, life will meet you there. But if you move like someone who already is—you will be.

I remind myself of this constantly: if I can see something, it's already mine.

A home I want to live in, a stage I want to stand on, an award I want to win—if I can visualize it, feel it, sense it in my bones, it means it exists. It means it's possible. So instead of letting old conditioning whisper, You could never, I answer with, I already am. When scarcity says, Must be nice, I reply, I can't wait. Because every time I speak it, I summon it. If I can see it—I can be it. And if I can be it, it's already on the way.

This is why it's important to protect your aura. To stay conscious of who and what you let into your mind, your home, your space. Because all of it—all of it—shapes your personality. And your personality shapes your personal reality.

How you be is what you get.

things I'm leaving behind in my never again era

As I move into the next chapter,
I'm packing light—
and throwing out what no longer belongs.

— Giving away my power
— Outsourcing the things that built me
— Rushing big decisions
— Ignoring my intuition
— Dismissing red flags
— Oversharing
— Giving my energy to people who haven't earned it
— Assuming everyone has my best interests at heart
— Trusting too quickly
— Staying loyal to old versions of me
— Apologizing for taking up space
— Performing just to be praised
— Analysis paralysis
— Abundance blocks like control and bitterness
— Staying in rooms where I feel unseen
— Chaos over clarity
— Entertaining low-vibe invitations just to feel included
— Waiting for permission
— Tolerating energy that drains me
— Dimming my light
— Seeking external validation
— Mistaking access for intimacy
— Getting lost in the "how"

Let this new era be my best one yet—
a full reclamation.
Where my boundaries are non-negotiable,
my truth is not up for debate,
and my past?
Exactly where I left it:
behind me.

THE HOLLAVERSE

"You should create your own world," she said. I leaned back in my chair as every hair on my body rose to the occasion. My brain spun like a turntable. My own world? I closed my eyes and asked to see it—no judgment, no rush, just trust. And then I did. A UFO-like vessel hovered above me, beaming down a hot pink light. I stepped into the center of it, looked up—and lifted off. I woke up in the HOLLAverse.

A world where art is oxygen, courage is currency, and self-expression reigns supreme. To my left, on a cosmic wall, bold graffiti flickered like prophecy. Beats blasted from a boombox, begging me to press play on a new way of being—a personal code of arms that vibrated like truth through my soul:

I create from soul, not mind.
I lead with intuition.
I respond, not react.
I relax into divine timing.
I age in flavor, not fear.
I create before I consume.
I share my art.
I am the dress code.
The mic is my sword.
My pen has power.
I am free. I am fire. I am art.
I am not a victim—I am the creator.
I attract the dopest souls on earth and beyond.
Abundance surrounds me.
Authenticity is my superpower.
Energy is sacred.
Access is earned.
I don't take advice from lives I wouldn't live.
I see fake energy and step out of its orbit.
I move toward joy—fast.
I don't wait. I declare.
I don't blend. I broadcast.
Courage is my crown.
Self-expression is my liberation.
And majesty? Is my birthright.

This is the HOLLAverse.

Welcome home.

THE SLEEPING PHOENIX

We're living through a revolution—one that experts say could rival the Industrial Revolution in scale and impact. But while that era was powered by machines, this one is powered by soul. The real transformation isn't just technological—it's energetic, creative, and deeply personal.

According to Human Design, we're approaching a once-in-a-400-year shift. The current global cycle—the Cross of Planning, which has emphasized structure, systems, and tribal safety—is coming to an end in 2027. We're entering a new era: the Cross of the Sleeping Phoenix. This shift marks the unraveling of old frameworks and the rise of self-sovereignty, individuality, and intuitive power.

It's not just a new chapter. It's an entirely new book.

The foundations we've relied on—institutions, governments, economic models—are evolving. And while AI and automation will continue reshaping our work, they won't replace our essence. Machines can assist. But they can't dream. They can't create meaning. They can't birth new paradigms. That belongs to you. Because unlike AI, you have a soul.

And that's the core of this revolution: not just change—but creative rebirth. A return to personal responsibility, energetic integrity, and self-expression as strategy. The world is calling for leaders and organizations that don't just talk about innovation—but create the conditions for it. Not through control or conformity—but through originality, imagination, and psychological safety.

The World Economic Forum ranks creativity and awareness among the top five most in-demand skills of the next decade. But those traits can't be downloaded—they must be unlocked. And they thrive in environments where people feel seen, supported, and safe enough to express.

That's where I come in.

If this speaks to your soul, scan this QR code and bring one of my keynotes to your next event.

Let's rehumanize the workplace—one bold self-expressionist at a time.

DESPITE ALL THE TURBULENCE,
ON THE FLIGHT OF HER LIFE,
SHE SAFELY LANDED.

AUDACITY

It's the secret sauce, the power move, the fire in your belly that dares to do what others won't. It's not about being reckless—it's about being relentlessly YOU.

Audacity is defined as intrepid boldness—the kind of gutsy, courageous spirit that doesn't just dream; it shows up and dares to make those dreams real. It's the confident disregard for the limitations society tries to throw on you. It's saying, "I see your rules, but I'm making my own."

And here's the truth: Without audacity, you'll stay stuck in the shadows of your own potential—caught in the safe, quiet space where nothing changes. Julia Cameron calls it being a "shadow artist." You're creative as hell, but you're not living it out loud. You're hiding, watching others do what you know you're meant to do—afraid to show up because you might get it wrong or look ridiculous. Or worse—you might actually succeed. And that's scary, too.

But I'm here to tell you that audacity is the only way out. It's not about faking it. It's about claiming it. You're not waiting for permission or perfection. You're moving, making noise, making mistakes, and being so damn good they can't ignore you. That's the vibe of audacity.

Audacity means dusting off your dreams and giving them a shot—even if your voice shakes, even if you're unsure. It's sharing your art on social media, even when the critics are circling. It's speaking on stage—even when your knees are knocking like Bambi. It's writing that book, launching that podcast, starting that business—because your soul says it's time.

The world needs your voice, your art, your unique flavor of greatness. It's time to come out of the dark and step into the light.

Be audacious. Be brave. Be undeniable.

Your magic doesn't belong in the shadows—it belongs in the spotlight.

LAZY AVOIDS PRESSURE

MEDIOCRE COMPLAINS ABOUT PRESSURE

ICONS APPLY PRESSURE

Can't stop.
Won't stop.
Always moving—
loud,
soft,
crash,
flow.
White caps rise,
blue rolls onto the shore,
making the world feel bigger,
better,
beyond me.
Its presence—a present.
Because isn't that what the ocean is designed to do?
To shift perspective—
on life,
on loss,
on everything we think we control.
So we stop playing detective,
knowing God's the director,
holding the script,
reminding us we're equipped—
for life's trips,
its dips,
and sharp left whips.
So sit with spirit.
Stay lit—knowing you are it.
and
ride the wave,
ride the wave,
ride the wave.

A LOVE LETTER TO YOU

Dear Wildly Dope Soul,

I hope your life is a symphony of chaos and champagne—equal parts hot mess and holy magic. I do hope you're embracing every hot flash, knowing that even though you miss things from the past, you're still on the right path. And by the way, if you're not having hot flashes yet—get excited. They are coming. But don't worry about aging, truly. It just keeps getting better and better as long as you're living and don't take yourself, or people's BS, or life too seriously. Because all that dirt? It only grows you into a flower, so keep stepping further and further into your power. Because it's that space between perfect and shit that makes you legit. And free—free to be who you came here to be. So trust and believe that all the best opportunities come from your struggle. Look, if it were easy, would it even be worth it? Probably not. So stay haute. And in case you forgot—and you better not—because you picked up this book, so clearly you're a fox: there is no wizard of Oz. It took Dorothy the entire freaking yellow brick road to figure out that the whole time she was actually it. And so are you. The power has been in your ruby-red soul the whole time. So stay lit. Stay fit. Stay in the way of it—it being your courage, your growth, your truth, always tapping into your own personal home. Because you are not alone. You're surrounded by other wildly dope souls. I just thought you should know.

xx,
J

—Written while sipping sangria on a rooftop in Nashville.

She's the sun.
She's the sky.
The phoenix that will rise.
She's the day.
She's the night.
The eagle mid-ascent in flight.
She's the ocean.
She's the flame.
The holy force that can't be named.
She's the stars.
She's the moon.
The map, the compass, the sacred tune.
Not half.
Not some.
She is all of it—
and then some.

FOR WHEN SHE FORGETS

I wrote this note to myself once before a big keynote.

My nerves were louder than my faith, and I needed something—anything—to bring me back to myself. I didn't know then that these words would become a lifeline. Now, I want to pass them on to you.

For the days when you doubt your voice.
For the moments before the mic goes hot or the Zoom light turns green.
For the quiet seconds when you forget who the hell you are.

Come back to this:

This isn't just a talk. This is a soul declaration. A mic-to-the-sky, heart-on-the-stage, full-body YES to the future you've been building—one messy, magical, creative rep at a time.

You've spent years—maybe even a lifetime—doing the invisible work: unlearning, shedding, listening to whispers that didn't make sense on paper, walking away from "safe" in favor of true. That's not just brave. That's leader energy. That's artist energy. That's the kind of presence that cracks open rooms.

So if your hands are shaking today? Good. It means you're not phoning it in. You're homing it in—straight from your soul to theirs. You're not giving a performance. You're creating a moment. You're reminding people what it looks like to show up real—and to be received as whole. Because this isn't just a keynote. It's a movement. And it's medicine for anyone in the room who's starving for resonance, for relief, for something real.

They don't just get slides today. They get you—unedited, unboxed, fully lit. And may I remind you: the talk is dope. The stories land. The framework hits. The presence is undeniable. You're not winging it. You're walking in—with soul, with prep, with power. So take the stage. Let your body lead. Let the art speak. Say what only you can say— in the way only you can say it.

And if you forget tomorrow? Come back here. Because your truth is not fragile. Your power doesn't expire. And your dreams have been waiting for you to show up like this.

HOLLER BACK

Look—you didn't make it this far in the book just to put it down and stay quiet. This book? It's not a one-time read. It's a return-to-remember kind of vibe. A mirror. A match. A call to go live.

So go. Be in your life. Make noise. Cause a ruckus. Because if you made it here, you already know—you've got more to give. And no, I don't mean in the hustle-harder, grind-til-you-bleed kind of way. That era's expired. Let her rest.

I mean in the drop-the-mask and show-me-who-you-are kind of way.

Sure, maybe you're still figuring it out. Welcome to the club. But here's the truth: you don't need to have it all figured out to make noise. You don't need a funnel or a five-year plan. You don't need anyone's playbook. You just need you—IRL. Artfully. Fully. Bravely.

Because no one can holler at your dreams for you. Because no one else is you. No one hears what you hear. Feels what you feel. Sees what you see when your eyes close and your soul starts talking.

So take the leap. Make the thing. Write the verse. Shake the room. Say the words. Paint it bold. Share it messy. Be misunderstood. Tell the truth.

You don't have to do it like them. You just have to do it like you.

Your life is your loudest piece. And your dreams? They're not gonna holler at themselves.

So get out there—and holler back.

She no longer phones it in.
She hones it in.
Ready to begin again—
but this time, from her soul within.
Silencing opinion.
Trusting her engine.
Catching attention.
No more apprehension.
She's steady in her reinvention,
bold with her divine intention.
No script. No mask. No pretension.
Just truth on loop, in full ascension.
A sacred calling.
A rhythm of stillness.
A strength that hums in quiet persistence.
A spell cast from intuition.

BE MORE YOU

Something happened that I'll talk about for the rest of my life. I was on a client customization call—the kind I've done hundreds of times over the last nine years as a keynote speaker. These are the calls where I get the intel I need to personalize the experience for the audience: who they are, what keeps them up at night, what they've loved (or not-so-much) about previous speakers.

Toward the end of the call, I asked a question I always ask: "What's worked in the past? What hasn't? What falls flat? What really crushes?" Everyone offered thoughtful feedback. And then one woman—who'd been quiet until then—unmuted and said, "I don't know if this will be valuable, but I'm just going to say it…"

She went on to tell me that throughout the history of this event, they've had many speakers take the stage. And everyone, she said, has had their thing: their energy, their wardrobe, their body language, their style. At this point, I braced myself. I assumed she was about to tell me to "tone it down" or not be "too much." I prepared for the whiplash of that all-too-familiar self-expression smack.

But then she said something I never saw coming: "So, Judi—whatever your thing is—be more of it. Bring more of it. Do all of it. That's what works. Be more YOU."

In all my years of doing these calls, no one has ever said that to me. I told her she'd just given me a gift. She created instant safety. She gave me full permission to self-express. And not just permission—encouragement. Expansion. Peace. By the way—this wasn't a casual gig. This was a high-stakes room of women in technology. My highest-profile audience to date. I was fully planning to deliver the safe talk—the one I knew would work. The one in my comfort zone. But because of her words, I didn't. I delivered the talk I really wanted to give. The one that came from my soul. And it worked. To be clear—this isn't about going rogue or being unfiltered. It's not about breaking rules just to make noise. It's about alignment—with yourself and with the space you're in.

True self-expression still honors the room. It respects context. It's not chaos—it's clarity. Because when people feel safe to fully express, they do their best, most original, most courageous work. They lead. They take initiative. They feel seen. And they want to stay.

This is the future of work: creativity, originality, and initiative. And it all starts with awareness—and environments that nurture the full expression of the humans inside them. Self-expression is the spark. Self-leadership keeps it safe. Courage is the crown. Let's build more of those rooms. Because that's how we holler at our dreams.

Expressionism isn't exclusive to art—
you are the art.

So in a world that feels like it's pulling us further and further apart,
maybe the glue that can put us back together
is you being you.
Not the system. Not the matrix.
Not the rules we break or obey.
But the brushstrokes of your presence—
the ultimate present.
The real gift.
The masterpiece.
As you master peace
by being who only you can be.
Because with every brave move you make,
you sign the canvas with your name.
Every moment,
every interaction—
a stroke of truth on the world's frame.
See, art isn't passive.
It moves.
   It speaks.
      It disrupts.
         It shakes.
Art doesn't sit back and wait.
   It dares.
      It does.
         It becomes.
            It picks up its pace.
So be the art.
And if you feel it in your gut—follow that.
If self-doubt shows up—shatter that.
If pride blocks your path—swallow that.
If confidence walks in—model that.
If you need to step back—honor that.
But if you lose your courage—call it back.

Because you'll never get in this life
what you aren't brave enough to HOLLER AT.

The Plot Twist
they didn't see it coming—
but she did.

READ THIS LAST

A love letter for the wildly dope soul who made it here.

This book almost didn't happen.

For years, I let other people's opinions mess with my mission. I was told the title was too much. I was told I was too much. And maybe you've been told the same.

For most of my life—especially as an entrepreneur—I've felt like an underdog. An outsider. Misunderstood. Overlooked. Boxed in. Some days, I swear I live on Lonely Island. And I think it's easy to look at someone online and assume they've got it all figured out. But I'm here to tell you: I don't. And I probably never will.

Because nobody knows shit about shit.

Sure, we gather wisdom. We evolve. We try our best. But deep down, I believe we create what we need. I wrote my first book about fear because I was one of the biggest scaredy cats you'd ever meet. Still am. I'm afraid of my own shadow some days—but I keep moving through it. On purpose. Daily. That's what makes me qualified to write about it. That's what makes me honest. That's what makes this real.

And I wrote this book because I needed to remember how to holler at my own dreams. To remember myself. To come back home.

This book saved me.

I almost let it die on the vine. I almost let it become something else—or nothing at all. Fear, doubt, anxiety, limiting beliefs, imposter syndrome, other people's opinions—cages. But creativity can't be caged. And truth can't be tamed. So here we are.

From the bottom of my wildly dope soul to the top of yours, I hope this book woke you, shook you, moved you, and reminded you: you are art. You are a miracle. Simply because you exist.

And your one life? It is so damn precious.

READ THIS LAST

The world needs your enthusiasm.
Your creativity.
Your courage.
Your essence.
Your confidence.
Your majic.
Your alignment.
Your originality.
Your self-expressionism.

There will be days ahead when people won't see you. Won't hear you. You'll have breakdowns and breakthroughs. You'll lose some. You'll win some. But if there's one thing I need you to remember, it's this:

When you hold your fear close,
give yourself grace,
and make faith your anchor—
you can't lose.

Because when you answer the call...
When you learn to sit with the pain...
Make peace with your path...
get present in your body...
And own who you truly are—
you shift. You soar. You rise into new paradigms.

And I believe God—Source—Spirit—whatever you believe in—rewards those who do.

So when you lose your way?
Pick this book up.
Fan the pages.
Let your eyes land where they're meant to.
Let that be your divine sign.

READ THIS LAST

When you feel like the world is against you—pick it up.
When you need a spark of creativity—pick it up.
When you want a vibe check—pick it up.
When someone you love forgets their magic—pass it on.

I love you. I see you. I am you.

Thank you for trusting me with your wildly dope soul. This book is now your sacred space. Come back as often as you need.

You are the masterpiece.

Now go paint your name all over the world's canvas.

Stay real—

xx

Judi Holler
Scottsdale, Arizona | June 2025

SNAPS

Thank you, God, for all these blessings. For this one wildly precious, dope life you've given me. For pulling me out of the darkness and into the light with this book you placed on my heart. I stand in awe of your grace.

Scott, I wrote the book! Thank you for being my ride-or-die, my biggest fan, my steady counsel, my real talk, my therapist, my safe place—and for reminding me who the f*ck I am every time I forget.

To my Daddio—for making me a Holler.

To my sister—for making me an aunt and giving me one of the most joyful, inspiring, and beautiful roles of my life.

To my soul sisters, Jodi and Noodle—you are my chosen family. Thank you for always cheering me on, keeping it real, and—most importantly—for letting me be safely me.

To the Fear Boss Fam—my OG's since the beginning. You know who you are.

To Ginger—your creativity, intuition, artistry, and entire vibe helped me bring this book to life in ways that can only be described as cosmic. 222!

To Sage—for waking up this beast.

To Jade—for gracing us with the present of your presence in this book. Your belief in me helped me believe in myself again—at a time when the light was dim and the path was unclear.

To Qveen, Human Design, Ghost Poetry Show, Aunt Dino, LCQ, Jenna, Tonya, The Mountain Mafia, YUCCA, Wehrle, Deets, Monster, Poola, Rosie, Niki, TT, Meg + Trip, Hainsworth House, Good Vibe Media, and Katie K.—for being portals of joy, creativity, and support as I made my journey back home.

It takes an army to launch a book—A heartfelt shout-out to Mission Driven Press, Amani Roberts, and the entire team at Book Launchers. Each of you were my book doulas, and I couldn't have done it without you.

To every single endorser at the front of this book who was selected with such deep intention and admiration. I am in awe of your dopeness.

SNAPS

To my glorious golden, Tito—who's laid at my feet through every word of every book. I hope this isn't our last one together, buddy... but if it is, what a way to go out. (And Jamo, my valiant guardian, I love you, too.)

To you—the reader. Without you, none of this works. You bring this book to life with every review, purchase, highlight, share, comment, like, and dog-eared page. Thank you for buying this book and trusting me with your one wildly dope soul.

Also? Because I can't help myself—and had to find a way to get Snoop in this book...

I wanna thank me.
I wanna thank me for doin' all this hard work.
For showing up when it would've been easier to scroll.
For setting the boundaries.
For staying focused.
For sitting my ass down and writing this book when I could've been in a pool. With a Cadillac.

I wanna thank me for not spiraling permanently.
For healing instead of hiding.
For walking away from what wasn't meant for me.
For trusting the vision before it made sense.
For not waiting on permission.
For remembering who TF I am—even when I forgot for a minute.

I wanna thank me for not quitting.
For keeping the faith when the plan fell apart.
For hollering at my dreams—even when they weren't hollering back.

Oh and ...
To anyone who ever doubted me: Your resistance became my revolution.

JOIN THE HOLLAVERSE

Want more HOLLA? Scan the QR code below to step into the HOLLAverse—a free, weekly, one-of-a-kind digital sanctuary for wildly dope souls like you.

This is where the book ends...
but the revolution begins.

Inside the HOLLAverse, you'll get:
- Fresh weekly writing + creative downloads
- Expressive prompts to stay lit and aligned
- First dibs on new merch, live events, book drops, and pop-ups
- VIP access to real-life experiences with me (yes, IRL!)
- Invitations to work with me—privately or on your big stage
- A monthly drop of what I'm loving, learning, and listening to

Whether you're here to feel more, create more, or be more YOU... this is your place. No algorithms. No filters. Just truth, creativity, and community. Around here, we don't chase dreams. We catch them.

Scan the code and let's keep this vibe alive.
Your inbox will never be the same.

Judi Holler is a creative entrepreneur, motivational speaker, and poet leading a revolution of Self-Expressionism—her bold, soul-driven approach to life and work. Born to HOLLER (literally), Judi helps people amplify their voice, unlock their creativity, and boldly chase what sets their soul on fire. Through performance, poetry, and the power of her pen, she inspires originality, courage, and radical self-expression. Whether on stage, on the page, or in your earbuds, Judi is here to remind you: You are the art. Your life is the canvas.

Join the movement at judiholler.com.

STAY REAL.

www.ingramcontent.com/pod-product-compliance
Lightning Source LLC
Chambersburg PA
CBHW072015170925
32745CB00002B/2